SO-BEZ-359

ANNA GRIFFIN

Paper Crafting with Elegance

ANNA  GRIFFIN

Paper Crafting with Elegance

HANDMADE PROJECTS
using RUBBER STAMPS, BRASS STENCILS,
DECOUPAGE AND SCRAPBOOK techniques

BY ANNA GRIFFIN

PLAID®

Editor: Mickey Baskett
Photographer: Jerry Mucklow
Art Director: Holley Silirie

All Night Media® is a registered trademark of Plaid Enterprises, Inc.
All Night Media products can be found at craft shops, stamping stores,
and department stores. For more information visit www.plaidonline.com.

Anna Griffin Incorporated is a manufacturer of exquisite paper products.
Find these products at gift shops, craft shops, stamping stores and
department stores.
*NOTE: All papers listed in the supply section of each project having product
numbers starting with "AG" are products from Anna Griffin Incorporated.*
To find a retailer who sells Anna Griffin papers, visit
www.annagriffin.com.

Disclaimer: The information in this instruction book is presented in
good faith, but no warranty is given, nor results guaranteed, nor is freedom
from any patent to be inferred. Since we have no control over physical
conditions surrounding the application of information herein contained,
Plaid Enterprises, Inc. disclaims any liability for untoward results.

IMPORTANT: Please be sure to thoroughly read the instructions for
all products used to complete projects in this book, paying particular
attention to all cautions and warnings shown for that product to
ensure their proper and safe use.

Copyright: All Rights Reserved. No part of this book may be reproduced
in any form without permission in writing, except by reviewer, who may in
reviewing this publication, quote brief passages in a magazine or newspaper.

© copyright 2003 by Plaid Enterprises, Inc.

Published by Plaid Enterprises, Inc.
3225 Westech Dr., Norcross, GA 30091-7600
www.plaidonline.com
800-842-4197
6/03

ISBN #1-55895-091-5

Printed in the U.S.A.

A Card-Making Dream Come True

One night while I was away at college, I had a remarkable dream about card making. It was such a powerful dream that I woke up in the middle of it and had to record all of the incredible images I saw. The cards were unique combinations of papers and elaborate design techniques. I was so excited by the dream that I stayed up half the night! I could tell then that this was a very significant moment in my life.

Here I am, years later, realizing that dream with this book. I am so lucky to be able to do what I love for a living, elegant paper crafting! My career and my company have grown out of that dream, so my advice to you is to pay attention to those moments of true inspiration.

I genuinely love making things, especially with paper. I hope this book inspires you to make glorious projects with paper, whether it be a simple card or an elegant scrapbook page. Each section of this book applies to a part of your life where paper crafting can be meaningful. I encourage you to stretch your imagination and incorporate paper crafts into your workspace, your home, and your life.

ACKNOWLEDGEMENTS

Special thanks and appreciation to Holley Silirie, Debby Schuh, Lisa Milam of Convivium Creative, Jen Mason, and Jenna Beegle for their never ending creativity. You are living proof that six heads are better than one! Thank you to Margaret Sunday, whose enthusiasm and support always keeps me going. Lastly, my sincere thanks to Mickey Baskett for the use of her beautiful home.

Contents

PAPER CRAFTING

1

materials

ENTER THE WORLD OF ANNA GRIFFIN'S DESIGNS, DERIVED FROM ANTIQUE ENGRAVINGS, EUROPEAN TEXTILES, AND HAND-PAINTED BOTANICALS — NOW AVAILABLE IN AN ARRAY OF PAPER CRAFTING PRODUCTS. USE WOOD-MOUNTED STAMPS, PUNCHES, BRASS EMBOSSING STENCILS, DECORATIVE PAPERS AND ACCESSORIES TO CREATE STUNNING CARDS, GIFTS, WRAPPINGS, AND SCRAPBOOK PAGES WITH ROMANTIC STYLE AND TIMELESS ELEGANCE.

RUBBER STAMPS AND INK

Anna Griffin Rubber Stamps by *All Night Media* feature solid hardwood mounts with contoured sides for a sure grip and precise placement. The exquisitely detailed designs are etched in quality rubber for a beautiful impression every time. There are six types of stamps: background, cartouche, salutation, alphabet, motif, and border. Combinations of stamps are available as sets.

Use **Background Stamps** to create all-over pattern, texture, and dimension. The **Cartouche** stamps come a variety of shapes and sizes. They act as frames or nameplates for stamping projects and work well with words, phrases, and initials. The **Salutations** stamps convey greetings and messages. Several styles of **Alphabet Stamps** can be used for messages and monogramming.

Motif stamps of botanicals and objects can be used alone or layered with backgrounds. **Border** stamps can be used for edgings, as frames, and as ornate stripes. They are designed to work as repeats on large projects like scrapbook pages and journals.

Anna Griffin **Pigment Ink Pads** create crisp, clear impressions. Each pad features a raised stamping surface to accommodate any size stamp. The high-quality archival ink is acid-free and fade resistant and comes in an array of beautiful colors.

BRASS STENCILS

Use **Anna Griffin Brass Stencils** from *All Night Media* to emboss elegant dimensional designs on paper quickly and easily. Designs include corners and motifs to use as central elements or for creating overall designs.

Use the stencils with the double-ended **Embossing Tool**, which has a larger tip for embossing open areas and a small tip for finely detailed designs.

Stencils are available individually and as kits that include a stencil, the Embossing Tool, and six cards with envelopes.

Satin Ribbon

Anna Griffin Double-faced Satin Ribbon from *All Night Media* is the perfect finishing touch for any project. It's easy to work with and comes in a variety of colors that coordinate with ink pad colors in 6mm and 18mm widths.

Punches

Anna Griffin Decorative Punches from *All Night Media* add intricate designs quickly and easily to your paper projects. Choose from corner designs and motifs. A hole punch is also handy to have to punch holes in the projects for threading ribbon.

Paper Goods

You can use a variety of papers for stamping and embossing. Many of the projects in this book feature decorative papers from *Anna Griffin Incorporated* that can be used alone or mixed together with coordinating stamped patterns. Be creative by cutting cut flowers or other motifs from printed papers, then layer the cutouts, adhering them with foam dots, to add dimension to your projects.

For decoupage, Anna Griffin has designed decoupage paper sets in Plaid's Royal Coat® line of products. These paper packs feature four coordinated papers in the set included design elements, background papers, and borders.

For small projects, you will need 1 piece of each of the papers listed in the individual project supply lists. If more paper is needed, it is indicated in the supply list.

NOTE: All papers listed in the supply section of each project having product numbers starting with "AG" are products from Anna Griffin Incorporated. To find a retailer who sells Anna Griffin papers, visit www.annagriffin.com.

Decorative Edge Scissors

Many projects in the book use decorative edge scissors to create a die cut effect. These scissors come in a variety of designs such as scallops, deckle, and others. Decorative edge scissors are widely available where craft products are found.

Pop Dots

Stamp Art™ Pop Dots *(from All Night Media)* are self-adhesive foam dots that are available in 1/2" diameter and 1/4" diameter. When placed under cut out paper motifs they raise the design above the surface and give a dimensional look to the design.

Adhesives

There are lots of wonderful adhesives for crafting available. Doublesided tape is used in many instances for gluing on cutouts and borders. When creating scrapbook pages, be sure to choose acid-free, archival quality adhesives.

Royal Coat® Decoupage Finish (1401) by *Plaid Enterprises, Inc.* is a glue and sealer in one that makes it easy to adhere sheets of paper and cutout motifs. Cloudy when applied, decoupage medium dries to a clear-hard finish. To apply, use a **foam brush**.

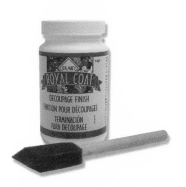

Other Materials

You'll also need these supplies for paper crafting:

- A **craft knife**, for making clean, straight cuts in papers and for cutting out intricate designs.
- A self-healing **cutting mat**, for cutting with a craft knife.
- A **steel ruler**, to use as a straight edge for cutting.
- A **triangle**, for making angle cuts.
- A pair of **scissors**, for trimming papers and cutting out motifs for decoupage and other projects.
- A soft-lead **pencil**, for marking measurements.
- A **stylus or bone folder** to aid in folding and creasing.

You may have other tools that make these projects easier to construct – feel free to use them.

PAPER CRAFTING

2

techniques

SOMETIMES, A LITTLE HELP
GOES A LONG WAY. FROM
RUBBER STAMPING IDEAS TO
TYING THE PERFECT BOW, SEE
HOW LEARNING A SIMPLE
TECHNIQUE CAN ADD
DRAMATIC IMPACT TO YOUR
PAPER PROJECTS.

How to Stamp

It is best to stamp on a flat, padded surface, such as a magazine or a stack of paper. This will ensure an even impression of the entire image. Start with a clean stamp. Practice first on scrap paper before you stamp your project.

1. Gently tap the pigment ink pad on the rubber side of the stamp, covering the stamp completely with ink.
2. Press the stamp carefully but firmly on your paper or card stock.
3. To prevent smearing, lift the rubber stamp straight up.

Tips:

• Make certain to apply even pressure to the stamp – the larger the stamp, the more pressure is required for a good impression.

• Don't rock the stamp! Rocking may produce back printing from extra ink picked up on the outside edges.

Cleaning Stamps: *Always* clean your stamp when changing ink colors. Use a stamp cleaner to remove the ink, then blot the stamp until dry on a paper towel.

Two Color Effects

You can create dramatic two color stamping effects using just one stamp. To do this, stamp one color at a time.

1. Cover the portion of the stamp you want to be the second color with a piece of paper.
2. Ink your stamp with the first ink color and stamp the image. Clean the stamp.
3. Repeat the process for the remaining portion of the stamp and the second ink color, carefully aligning the stamp.

Masking a Stamp

Many times you will want to print only part of the stamp. When you do, mask off parts of the stamped image with sticky notes. (This is a bit tricky, so you might want to practice on scrap paper before you try it on your project.) This example shows how to create a mitered-corner border with a stamp.

1. Position the sticky note on the area of the paper on which you don't want the image to be printed. Stamp the image. As you can see, part of the image is stamped on the sticky note.
2. Remove the sticky note to reveal the masked area.
3. To continue, use another sticky note to cover part of the area already stamped as to not get an

overlapping image. Add another sticky note at the next corner where the border will continue.

4. Stamp the image. Part of the image appears on the sticky note that masks off the area.

5. When the mask is removed, you have mitered corners.

Heat Embossing

Heat embossing adds texture and polish to stamp art. Use embossing powder (available in clear, metallic, glitter, and solid) and an embossing heat tool to produce a shiny, raised finish. Here's how:

1. Stamp the design with ink.
2. Before the ink dries, pour embossing powder generously over the stamped image. Tap off excess powder over a folded piece of paper (so it's easy to pour the powder back in the jar).
3. Heat the image for about 10 seconds with an embossing heat tool, such as the All Night Media Heat It® Craft Tool (37HET). You will see the powder melt and turn into a shiny, raised image.

Paper Punching

Paper punching is a great way to make intricate cuts in paper quickly and easily.

1. Place the punch on a firm surface.
2. Slide the paper or card stock between the punch blades.
3. Press down on the top of the punch until the paper pops out.
- For best results, lubricate the punch by punching a piece of wax paper.
- To sharpen and clean your punch, punch through aluminum foil.
- To position a punch exactly, turn the punch over and align with the base up.

Embossing with Brass Stencils

Brass stencils can create elegant, embossed, dimensional designs on paper quickly and easily.

1. Position the stencil on a light box or light source. Secure the card stock face down on the stencil. For best results, use a low tack adhesive.

2. Rub wax paper over the paper surface to lubricate.
3. Trace over the stencil design with the Anna Griffin Embossing Tool, applying pressure along the edges of the cutout areas of the stencil. Repeat, if necessary.
4. When all areas are embossed, remove the stencil and turn over the card.

For a debossed (recessed) effect, use the side of the card with depressions rather than the raised, or embossed side.

Decoupage

Decoupage is a wonderful way to decorate with motifs and pattern. Here are the steps to successful decoupage. To begin, surfaces should be clean, smooth, and dry.

1. Plan your project. Cut out motifs from paper with scissors or a craft knife. Arrange the print(s) on the surface to plan the placement before you apply decoupage medium.

2. Place the cutout(s) face down on wax paper. Working one cutout at a time, brush decoupage medium

on the back of the print.

3. Lift the cutout and position it on the surface. Working from the center outward, press gently with your fingers or a soft cloth to work out any air bubbles. Be sure the edges are adhered well.

4. Clean up area around the print with a damp sponge or paper towel. Let dry completely before proceeding.

5. To finish, apply a thin coat of decoupage medium to cover the project surface. Let dry. Apply a second coat; let dry completely.

• When dry, the surface will be clear, not milky or cloudy.

• Brush on thin coats, not thick coats.

• If the surface feels tacky, let dry longer.

• When layering designs, allow the first layer to dry completely before applying the second layer.

REVERSE DECOUPAGE

Reverse decoupage is a way to add images to glass surfaces so the image can be seen through the glass. In planning your design, place the images that are in the front of the design first and those in the background later.

1. Apply decoupage medium to the printed (right) side of a paper cutout.

2. Press the printed side of the cutout against the glass surface. Smooth the cutout, removing air bubbles. Use a damp sponge or paper towel to remove excess decoupage medium from the glass. Let dry.

3. Add other cutouts to finish the design, repeating the process in step 2. Let dry.

4. Paint entire surface and cutout with coordinating acrylic paint color(s) *or* cover the entire area with paper, using decoupage medium to apply the paper to the surface. Let dry.

5. Seal with one to two coats of decoupage medium.

Caution: Do not place prints on the side of glass dishes or glassware where foods or liquids may touch them

USING A CRAFT KNIFE

Use a craft knife for precision cutting on your craft projects. For precise straight cuts, work on a cutting mat, hold the knife like a pencil, and drag it towards you, following the edge of a metal ruler.

• Always cut toward your body to maintain control over the knife.

• A good, sharp blade is essential for neat edges, so change the blade frequently.

• Always keep knives and blades out of the reach of children.

SCORING AND CREASING

Scoring paper and card stock makes it much easier to fold. To make crisp folds, you need a straight edge, a stylus, and a bone folder.

1. Place the straight edge where you want the fold to be. Score the line with the stylus. (You could also use the Embossing Tool, the pointed end of the bone folder, a butter knife, or an empty ballpoint pen.)

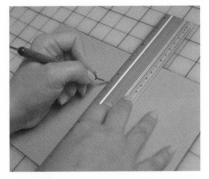

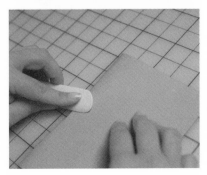

2. Fold the card along the scored line. Using the rounded end of the bone folder, run it along the fold to make a crisp crease.

PAPER PLEATING

Pencil pleating is a paper folding technique that creates even pleats in one direction.

1. Using a ruler and a pencil, measure and make light pencil marks on the back of the paper at 5/8" and 3/8" increments along top and bottom of areas to be pleated.

2. Using a straight edge and a stylus, score the lines, placing the straight edge at the marks.
3. Fold back and forth, making an accordion fold.

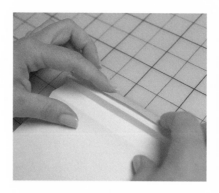

MITERING CORNERS

Mitering joins two strips of paper together, creating a 45 degree diagonal line at the right-angle corner where the two strips meet. This is the technique used to make paper frames. To start, cut the strips of paper the width and length needed to create the frame.

1. Glue the strips together at a right angle, overlapping the ends. Either use a repositionable glue or work quickly to create the miter before the glue dries.

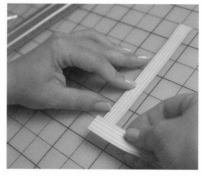

2. Position a straight edge diagonally across the corner. With a craft knife, cut through both pieces from the inside corner to the outside corner.

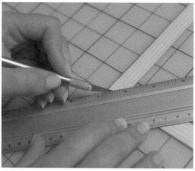

3. Remove the triangles of paper on the top and bottom where the strips overlap.

MAKING AN ENVELOPE

You can make envelopes to fit any size card. Use glue or double-sided tape to seal the top flap of the envelope after you insert the card.

1. Measure your card and add 1/2" to 1" to the height and width. (This is your base size.)
2. Add the bottom flap, which is three-fourths of the envelope base height plus 1".
3. Add the top flap, which is one-fourth of the base height plus 1".
4. Add the side flaps, which are 1".
5. Taper all flaps slightly.
6. Mark the fold lines and score,

using a ruler and a bone folder or the Embossing Tool.

7. Fold in the side flaps. Apply glue to the edges of the bottom flap and fold over the side flaps. Fold down the top flap.

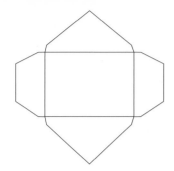

Making an envelope liner

It's easy to make a custom decorative envelope liner. The liner should fit just below the glue line of the envelope.

1. Cut a piece of paper just slightly smaller than the size of the open envelope to use as a pattern. Check the fit.

2. Trace around the pattern on the liner paper. Cut out. (It's best to use a straight edge and a craft knife.)

3. Decorate the liner to match the card – use coordinating stamps and ink colors or decorative paper.

4. Slide the liner in the envelope to check the fit and the look.

5. Remove the liner. Add adhesive to the top back edge and replace inside the envelope, pressing to adhere to the flap.

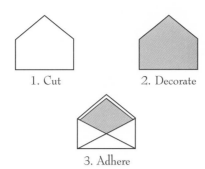

1. Cut   2. Decorate

3. Adhere

Tying a bow

Create the perfect finishing touch with the the perfect bow:

1. Create ribbon loop and hold it in your left hand with your thumb, with the loop facing the ceiling.

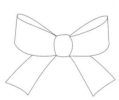

2. With the shorter end in front, pointing towards your wrist, place the long end of the ribbon over the back and up and over your hand.

3. Push a loop from the long end behind the first loop and through itself. Pull left and right side loops tight while holding down the streamers to create a symmetrical bow. Adjust streamers and pull bow tight to finish. Trim the ribbon ends.

Tying a Square Knot

Wrap ribbon in place around card or project. Cross right end over left, push under the left side, and pull up. Cross top end over bottom end. Push up through loop. Pull ends taught and trim.

Tying a Threaded Knot

1. Punch two holes about 1/4" apart on your card or surface. Cut a piece of ribbon.
2. Thread each end of the ribbon down through separate holes on the front side. Cross ribbons in the back and feed ends back through the front of the card.
3. Pull the ends taught and trim.

Dovetail Ribbon Ends

Dovetailing is a decorative way to finish a bow or knotted ribbon. After tying the bow or knot, fold the ends of the ribbon in half horizontally. Trim folded ribbon at an angle, approximately 1" in from the end. Unfold for the dovetail effect.

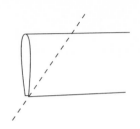

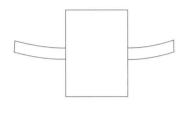

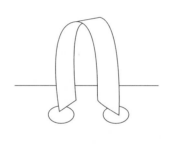

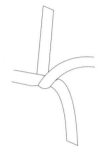

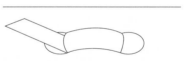

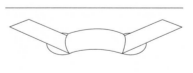

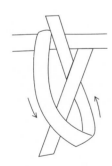

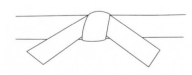

IAGRAMS

Use the following diagrams to create templates for some of the projects in this book.

Pillow Box, page 23

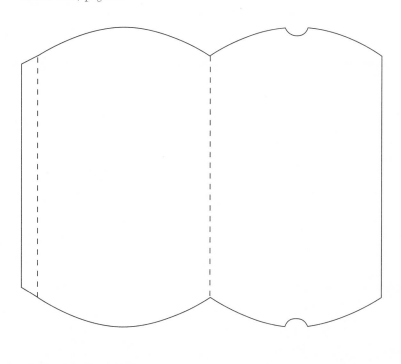

Old Friends Card, page 23

Folded Gift Bag, page 63

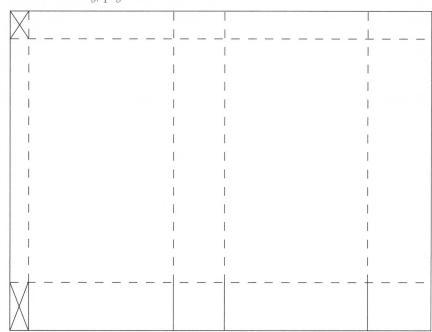

CD Envelope, page 87

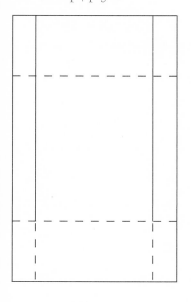

PAPER CRAFTING

3

for keeping in touch

HANDMADE CARDS AND
ANNOUNCEMENTS AFFORD
SPECIAL WAYS TO SAY "I
MISS YOU," "THANK YOU," AND
"I LOVE YOU," THEY ARE A
LOVELY WAY TO ANNOUNCE A
WEDDING OR BIRTH OR
OFFER HOLIDAY GREETINGS.
YOU CAN ALSO USE CARD-
MAKING TECHNIQUES TO
CREATE PERSONALIZED
STATIONERY FOR NOTES AND
LETTERS.

OLD FRIENDS CARD

This card combines elegant stamping with a delicate bow and a classic phrase for a dear friend. Your sentiments become even more magical when presented in this special way.

YOU WILL NEED

Anna Griffin Products by All Night Media®

"THE BEST MIRROR..." SALUTATION STAMP 580D05

SWAG CARTOUCHE STAMP 580K05

REPOUSSE BACKGROUND STAMP 580K06

PURPLE INK PAD 19APR

GREEN INK PAD 19AGR

GREEN SATIN RIBBON 93GRN

Paper

GREEN PAPER AG016*

PURPLE PAPER AG033*

IVORY CARD STOCK, 2 PIECES 8-1/2" X 11"

VELLUM

Other Supplies

DECORATIVE EDGE SCISSORS

ADHESIVES OF YOUR CHOICE

CRAFT KNIFE

HOLE PUNCH

Products by Anna Griffin Inc.

DIRECTIONS

The Card

1. Cut a 7-3/4" x 4-1/2" rectangle of ivory card stock. Score and fold in half to make a 3-7/8" x 4-1/2" folded card.

2. Trim a rectangle of purple paper to 3-1/2" x 4-1/4". Cut another piece to 1-3/4" x 2".

3. Trim a vellum rectangle to 3-1/2" x 3".

4. Cut a 3-1/2" x 4" green paper rectangle. Use the Repousse Background stamp with Purple ink to stamp a background pattern. Let dry. Trim the edges with decorative edge scissors.

5. Cut a piece of ivory card stock to 1-1/2" x 1-3/4". Stamp "The Best Mirror" stamp in the center with Green ink.

6. Layer and adhere the cut rectangles to the front of the folded card in this order: the large lavender piece, the green stamped piece, the vellum, the small lavender piece, and the small stamped ivory piece.

The Wrapping:

1. Cut a piece of card stock to 7-1/2" x 4-1/2". Measure and mark this piece 1-1/2" in from each end. Score and fold where marked.

2. Stamp the 1-1/2" ends using the Swag stamp with Purple ink.

3. Using a craft knife, trim the ends around the stamped areas into half circle shapes.

4. Punch a hole in each side of the rounded ends for the ribbon.

5. Place the completed, signed card in the wrapping. Lace a 6" piece of ribbon through the punched holes and tie in a bow.

THE BEST
MIRROR IS
AN OLD
FRIEND.

—GEORGE
HERBERT

FANCY FLORAL CARDS

Here's a beautiful way to express your thanks.

OU WILL NEED

Anna Griffin Products
by All Night Media®

STARTER STAMP GIFT SET 5809SK -
(TULIP, FLORAL, "THANK YOU"
STAMPS)

GREEN INK PAD 19AGR

CRIMSON INK PAD 19ABG

GREEN SATIN RIBBON 93GRN

Paper

GREEN PATTERNED PAPER AG073*

IVORY CARD STOCK, 3 PIECES
8-1/2" X 11"

Other Supplies

HOLE PUNCH

ADHESIVES OF YOUR CHOICE

Products by Anna Griffin Inc.

IRECTIONS

1. Cut ivory card stock to 9" x 6". Score and fold in half.

2. Trim another piece of ivory card stock, tearing the edges, to 2-1/2" x 5-1/4". Stamp a pattern on the piece, using the Floral motif stamp with Crimson ink.

3. Cut a piece of green patterned paper to 5-3/4" x 4-1/8". Tear edges.

4. Adhere the green piece, centering it, on the front of the folded card. Adhere the stamped crimson patterned piece, using the photo as a guide.

5. Cut a piece of ivory card stock to 4" x 1-1/2". Stamp, using the Tulip motif stamp with Green ink.

6. Stamp "Thank You" in Green ink under the tulip.

7. Punch a hole in the top of the tulip piece and another in the top of the card front.

8. Secure tulip piece to the card with ribbon. Tie a bow.

Send a message of love with this elegant floral card.

OU WILL NEED

Anna Griffin Products
by All Night Media®

STARTER STAMP GIFT SET 5809SK -
(FLORAL AND "LOVE" STAMPS)

GREEN INK PAD 19AGR

CRIMSON INK PAD 19ABG

Paper

GREEN PATTERNED PAPER AG003*

GREEN PATTERNED PAPER AG039*

FLORAL PAPER AG024*

IVORY CARD STOCK, 2 PIECES
8-1/2" X 11"

Other Supplies

POP DOTS™ ADHESIVE FOAM DOTS
(ALL NIGHT MEDIA, 73DOT)

ADHESIVES OF YOUR CHOICE

Products by Anna Griffin Inc.

IRECTIONS

1. Cut ivory card stock to 6-7/8" x 4-3/8". Score and fold 2-1/2" from left edge so the front of the card is about half the width of the back.

2. Cover the inside panel of the card with floral paper.

3. Cover the front half panel of the card with green patterned paper (AG003).

4. Cut three 1-1/4" squares of ivory card stock.

5. Stamp the floral motif stamp with Green ink on two squares.

6. Stamp "Love" with Crimson ink on the other square.

7. Cut three 1-1/2" squares of green patterned paper (AG039). Adhere these to the front of the card so half the square hangs over the half front panel.

8. Adhere the stamped squares on the green patterned squares, using foam dots.

tured left to right: Floral Thank You Card, Floral Love Card

WINDOWS OF LOVE CARD

A delicate cutout cartouche hangs in the window of the front of this card.

 OU WILL NEED

*Anna Griffin Products
by All Night Media®*

STARTER STAMP GIFT SET 5809SK -
(CARTOUCHE, FLORAL, AND "LOVE"
STAMPS)

GREEN INK PAD 19AGR

BLACK INK PAD 19ABK

Paper

BLUE PATTERNED PAPER AG045*

IVORY CARD STOCK

Other Supplies

POP DOTS™ FOAM ADHESIVE DOTS
(ALL NIGHT MEDIA, 73DOT)

ADHESIVES OF YOUR CHOICE

Products by Anna Griffin Inc.

*D*IRECTIONS

1. Cut ivory card stock to 9" x 6". Score and fold in half to make a card 4-1/2" x 6".

2. Cut a piece of blue patterned paper 4-1/4" x 5-3/4". Adhere to the front of the card.

3. Cut a window in the front of the card 2-1/2" x 2". Reserve the cut piece.

4. Trim the cut-out window piece to 2-1/4" x 1-3/4". Stamp a pattern using the Floral motif stamp with Green ink. Adhere this piece inside the card so it shows through the window on the front.

5. Stamp the Cartouche on ivory card stock with Green ink.

6. Stamp "Love" at the center of the cartouche with Black ink. Cut out the cartouche.

7. Stamp the Floral motif stamp on ivory card stock with Green ink. Cut it out.

8. Cut a thin strip of blue paper and use it to suspend the "Love" cartouche in front of the window. Adhere with the cutout floral motif and a foam dot.

HOLIDAY PAPER GARLAND

This holiday card is a Christmas keepsake – a garland greeting that
can be hung on the mantle or on a tree.

You WILL NEED

*Anna Griffin Products
by All Night Media®*

GREEN SATIN RIBBON 93GRN

Paper

POINSETTIA PAPER AG106*

HOLLY PAPER AG105*

DARK GREEN PATTERNED PAPER
    AG051*

RED PAPER AG028*

SAGE GREEN SUEDE PAPER

INKJET MATTE PHOTO PAPER

Other Supplies

ROUND HOLE PUNCH, 1/8"

ROUND BRASS GROMMETS, 1/8"

GROMMET SETTER

3 PHOTOS

COMPUTER WITH SCANNER AND
    INKJET PRINTER

ADHESIVES OF YOUR CHOICE

*Products by Anna Griffin Inc.

Directions

Photo Squares

1. Print each photo 2" square on matte photo paper. Cut out each 3-1/4" square allowing 5/8" white space around sides.

2. On each photo square, measure 5/16" from the right and left edges and mark with a small dot. Be sure the mark is centered from top to bottom. Set aside.

3. Cut out three 4-1/4" squares – one from holly paper and two from poinsettia paper. Set aside.

4. Cut out three 4-3/4" squares – one from red paper and two from the dark green patterned paper.

5. Layer and adhere the squares starting with the solid paper, then patterned paper. End with the photo on top.

6. Using the marked dots on the photo squares as guides, punch six holes with a 1/8" hole punch.

7. Place a brass grommet through each hole from front to back and secure with a grommet setter.

Text Rectangles

1. Compose a four-panel message (this one is "wishes" "&" "kisses" plus a signature panel) for your card. Print or write each part of the message inside a 3" x 1" rectangle, leaving 5/8" of white space on each end.

2. On each text rectangle, measure 5/16" from the right and left edges and mark with a small dot, centering the marks top to bottom. Set aside.

3. Cut out four 3-1/2" x 1-1/2" rectangles from sage suede paper.

4. Layer and adhere a text rectangle on each suede rectangle.

5. Punch holes and add grommets.

Assembly

1. Cut a 48" piece of sage satin ribbon.

2. Lay out the seven completed shapes in order beginning with the first text rectangle, then the first photo square. Alternate rectangles and squares, ending with the square signature panel.

3. Tie a knot in one end of the ribbon about 1-1/2" from the end.

4. Starting with the first rectangle, thread the ribbon from top to bottom through the left grommet. Bring the ribbon up through the right grommet of the rectangle. Slide the rectangle all the way down the ribbon to the end, leaving 3" between the rectangle and the tied knot. Repeat this step with each shape, leaving the same amount of space between each. Tie a knot in the other end of the ribbon and hang the garland.

WISHES

KISSES

THE GARRE
WILL, KELLY, ADELINE &

WISHES

HAND EMBOSSED CARD

Layering embossed and punched papers makes an elegant card.

YOU WILL NEED

Anna Griffin Products
by All Night Media®

DAMASK BRASS STENCIL 5800S

FLEUR DE LIS PUNCH 59FDL

EMBOSSING TOOL 5806ST

Paper

PLATINUM PAPER AG010*

GREEN PAPER AG016*

GREEN VELLUM AG240*

IVORY CARD STOCK

Other Supplies

IVORY WIRE-EDGE RIBBON, 1-1/2" X 9"

VERSAMARK WATERMARK INK PAD
    (ALL NIGHT MEDIA , 33WTR)

HOLE PUNCH

ADHESIVES OF YOUR CHOICE

Products by Anna Griffin Inc.

DIRECTIONS

1. Cut ivory card stock to 5-1/2" x 11" and green vellum to 5" x 10-1/2". Score and fold to make a square card. Layer the vellum over the card stock.

2. Punch two holes in the top front of the card through both layers and secure with a bow.

3. Cut a piece of green paper 4-5/8" x 4-5/8". Cut a piece of platinum paper 4-1/2" x 4-1/2".

4. Punch the corners of the platinum paper square with the Fleur De Lis punch and adhere to the green paper square.

5. Punch 10 Fleur de Lis motifs from scraps of green paper and adhere around the border of the platinum paper, using the photograph at right as a guide for placement. Adhere to the card.

6. Using the Damask stencil, emboss a 2-3/4" x 3" piece of platinum paper.

7. Rub the inkpad lightly across the surface of the embossing to create an aged effect.

8. Mount the embossed piece on a 3" x 3-1/4" piece of ivory card stock and adhere on the card.

PERSONALIZED STATIONERY BOX SET

Make an elegant fold-out box with compartments for paper and envelopes. Custom made stationery is a perfect gift for yourself or for a dear friend.

OU WILL NEED

*Anna Griffin Products
from All Night Media®*

ANTIQUE ALPHABET STAMP SET
2480P

STARTER STAMP SET 5809SK - FLORAL
MOTIF STAMP

GREEN SATIN RIBBON 93GRN

GREEN INK PAD 19AGR

Paper

FLORAL PAPER AG024*, 4 SHEETS

GREEN PATTERNED PAPER AG118*

GREEN PAPER AG016*

PLAIN ENVELOPES TO FILL BOX

WRITING PAPER, 6" X 8-1/2" TO FILL
BOX AND TO LINE ENVELOPES

Other Supplies

CHIPBOARD

ROYAL COAT® DECOUPAGE FINISH
(1401)

FOAM BRUSH

ADHESIVES OF YOUR CHOICE

Products by Anna Griffin Inc.

IRECTIONS

Cutting the Box

1. From chipboard, cut the pieces for the inner box front:
   One 6-3/4" x 2" (for the front)
   Two 3/8" x 2" (for the sides)
   One 1-1/2" x 6-3/4" (for the base)
2. From chipboard, cut pieces for the inner box middle:
   One 6-3/4" x 4" (for the front)
   Two 3/8" x 4" (for the sides)
3. From chipboard, cut pieces for the inner box rear:
   • One 6-3/4" x 6"
   • Two 1/4" x 6"
4. From chipboard, cut the cover:
   • Two 9-1/2" x 3-1/2" (for the fronts)
   • Two 9-1/2" x 1-1/2" (for the sides)
   • One 9-1/2" x 7" (for the back)

Making the Cover

1. To cover the outside of the cover, use two pieces of floral paper. Cut one piece in half and reverse it to create the pattern on the front. For the fronts, cut two pieces 6" x 10-1/2". For the back, cut a piece 12" x 10-1/2".
2. First, cover the front panels using decoupage finish as the adhesive. On each sheet, 1/2" in from the bottom edge and front edge, adhere one 3-1/2" x 9-1/2" piece of chipboard. (Remember to make these mirror images.) Leave a gap of 3/8" and adhere the 1-1/2" x 9-1/2" strips of chipboard. Leave another 3/8" gap, then adhere the back piece of chipboard (9-1/2" x 7".) Use the remaining piece of floral paper to cover it, letting the ends overlap the sides.
3. Trim corners on the diagonal and fold edges down over the chipboard. Adhere in place. Crease the lining papers firmly in the gaps between the chipboard pieces while the glue is still wet for a better, more secure joint.
4. Cut the ribbon in half. Secure a piece on the inside of each front piece. Leave about 1" of ribbon attached to the chipboard, with the rest hanging free to make the front closure.
5. Cut two pieces of green paper 9-3/8" x 6". Use them to line the inside of the front covers (covering the ends of the ribbon) and sides. Adhere securely.
6. Cut a piece of floral paper 7" x 9-3/8" to line the center back inside. Adhere securely. Let dry.

Making the Inside Boxes

1. Using the chipboard pieces of the inside boxes listed above, attach the sides of the rear box to its front. Repeat for the middle box.
2. For the front box, attach the sides to the front, then add the base. This base is for all of the boxes. It will be covered with the same paper as the front.

Covering the Boxes

1. Cover the back box with a piece of floral paper 8-3/4" x 6-1/2".
2. Cover the middle box with a piece of green patterned paper 8-3/4" x 4-1/2".
3. Cover the front box and bottom with a piece of floral paper 8-3/4" x 4".
4. Adhere the boxes to the base. Let dry thoroughly.
5. Add box assembly to the back center of the cover.

Stamping the Stationery

1. For the stationery, stamp an initial, using an Alphabet stamp with Green ink at the top of the paper.
2. Stamp with Floral Motif stamp under the initial with Green ink.
3. Add stationery to box.

Lining the Envelopes

1. Cut paper to line the envelopes. Slip inside and secure.
2. Place envelopes in the box.

GARLAND-IN-A-BOX BABY ANNOUNCEMENT

Here's a special way to herald an auspicious arrival. One side of the card garland spells
B-A-B-Y; the other side announces the vital statistics.

You will need

*Anna Griffin Products
by All Night Media®*

LATTICE BORDER STAMP 580H06

FILIGREE ALPHABET STAMP SET
2485P

PINK INK PAD 19APK

PINK SATIN RIBBON 93PNK

Paper

FLORAL PAPER AG012*

IVORY PAPER

Other Supplies

CLEAR EMBOSSING POWDER
(ALL NIGHT MEDIA (36CLR)

PAPIER MACHÉ BOX, 2" SQUARE

ROYAL COAT® DECOUPAGE FINISH
(1401)

FOAM BRUSH

POP DOTS™ ADHESIVE FOAM DOTS
(ALL NIGHT MEDIA, 73DOT)

ADHESIVES OF YOUR CHOICE

*Products by Anna Griffin Inc.

Directions

Wrapping the Outside of the Box

1. From ivory paper, cut one 4" square
   and one 5" square.
2. Stamp the Lattice Border stamp with
   Pink ink on each side of each square
   so the tops of the borders meet in
   the centers of the squares. Emboss
   with clear embossing powder.
3. Place the squares face down. Center
   the box top on the smaller square
   and the box base on the larger
   square. On two sides, cut slits from
   edge of the paper to the edge of the
   box. Cover the box base and lid with
   the paper, tucking the paper over
   the edges to the inside, Adhere with
   decoupage finish.

Lining the Box

1. From floral paper, cut one 3" square
   and one 4" square.
2. Position the lid on the 3" square and
   the box base on the 4" square.
   Notch the corners. (This makes it
   easier to tuck the paper in the box.)
3. Adhere the box base liner to the box.
4. Cut a 12" piece of ribbon. Cut a slit
   in the center of the lid liner the
   same width as the ribbon. Feed 1/4"
   of ribbon through the liner, allowing
   the rest to hang through on the
   patterned side of the paper. Anchor

the short end (it will be hidden).
Attach the liner to the lid.

Making the Card

*You can use a computer to print the text
of your announcement on ivory paper and
then cut out the squares, or you can
handwrite the text after you cut the
squares, as these directions indicate.*

1. Cut eight 1-1/4" squares from the
   ivory paper.
2. Using pink ink and clear embossing
   powder, stamp the letters to spell
   "BABY" on four squares with
   Filigree Alphabet stamps.
3. On the other four squares, add the
   text of the announcement (name,
   date, weight, length).
4. Cut eight 1-1/2" floral paper
   squares. Adhere ivory squares on
   the floral squares, using foam dots.
5. Adhere the squares on the ribbon
   hanging from the lid, matching a
   text square on one side of the
   ribbon with a stamped square on
   the other side.
6. Cut the ends of the ribbon in a
   dovetail.

BASSINET BABY ANNOUNCEMENT

A crib with a pleated pink skirt announces the birth of a baby girl. Of course, for a boy you could make it in blue and use the "It's a Boy!" Stamp.

You WILL NEED

*Anna Griffin Products
by All Night Media®*

"IT'S A GIRL!" STAMP 580D02

PINK INK PAD 19APK

Paper

PINK PATTERNED PAPER AG083*

PINK PATTERNED PAPER AG085*

DIE CUT BIRDS AND FLOWERS AG524*

Other Supplies

THIN WHITE CORDING, 6"

HOLE PUNCH

ADHESIVES OF YOUR CHOICE

To create an announcement for a boy, use:

BLUE INKPAD 19ABL

BLUE PAPERS AG062 & AG058

"IT'S A BOY" STAMP 580D01

*Products by Anna Griffin Inc.

DIRECTIONS

Making the Card

1. Cut 7-1/2" x 4" strip from pink patterned paper (AG083). Score and fold in center to create a card with the fold to the left.

2. With card closed, measure 2-1/8" in from the right side of the card and 1-3/8" down from the upper edge of the card. Cut off that corner. (This is the opening of the bassinet.) Cut the curved hood of the bassinet.

Making the Bassinet Skirt

1. Cut a strip of pink patterned paper (AG083) 8" x 2-1/2". Measure and mark from left side across top at every 1/4" and every 1" mark.

2. Score paper at the measurements and fold. Fold each end back, then each pleat forward. Adhere pleats together at top of skirt with double-sided adhesive.

3. Adhere to the card along the top edge of the pleats and at each end of the skirt.

4. Cut 1/4" x 3-3/4" and 1/4" x 1-3/8" strips from pink patterned paper (AG085). Adhere along top edge of skirt and hood of bassinet, using photo as a guide.

Decorations

1. Stamp "It's A Girl" with pink ink on ivory card stock. Cut to make a tag 1-1/8" x 3/4". Punch a hole and add cording.

2. Adhere die cut flowers and birds to card as shown.

PAPER CRAFTING 4

for gift giving

GIVING IS A PLEASURE WHEN
IT COMES FROM THE HEART.
YOU CAN USE YOUR PAPER
CRAFTING SKILLS TO CREATE A
VARIETY OF MEMORABLE GIFTS.
THIS SECTION INCLUDES IDEAS
AND INSTRUCTIONS FOR MAK-
ING DECORATED JOURNALS,
COVERED BOXES, FRAMES, AND
CONTAINERS FOR PLANTS AND
FLOWERS.

JUST FOR YOU JOURNAL & SHADOW BOX FRAME

A layered floral cover makes a wire-bound journal a thoughtful hand crafted gift.

 **OU WILL NEED**

*Anna Griffin Products
by All Night Media®*

GREETINGS STAMP SET 2484R - "JUST
   FOR YOU" STAMP

PINK SATIN RIBBON 93PNK

Paper

PINK FLORAL PAPER AG108*

BROWN PATTERNED PAPER AG110*

DIE CUT FLOWERS AG521*

FRAME PAGE AG703*

JOURNAL PAGE AG712*

Other Supplies

STAMP-A-MEMORY INK PAD - SOFT
   WHEAT (ALL NIGHT MEDIA 22SWH)

STAMP ART FRAME JOURNAL (ALL
   NIGHT MEDIA 87FJL)

POP DOTS™ ADHESIVE FOAM DOTS
   (ALL NIGHT MEDIA, 73DOT)

ADHESIVES OF YOUR CHOICE

Products by Anna Griffin Inc.

 **IRECTIONS**

1. Cut 5" x 6-1/2" from pink floral paper. Cut window from paper to match window in journal cover. Adhere paper on journal cover.

2. Cut frame from Frame Page (AG703), adhering in place over the window with foam dots.

3. Adhere die cut flowers to side of window with foam dots

4. Cut a piece of brown patterned paper 1/2" x 6-1/2". Adhere on cover 1/8" from left side.

5. Cut label from journal page (AG712). Stamp "Just for You" with Soft Wheat ink.

6. Place label on brown patterned paper. Trim, leaving a narrow border. Adhere to journal cover.

7. Cut out leaves and flowers from pink floral paper and adhere with foam dots.

8. Cut a piece of pink satin ribbon to use as a bookmark and attach inside journal.

Paper cutouts are layered inside the paper-covered mat of a shadow box frame to make a charming piece of wall art.

 **OU WILL NEED**

*Anna Griffin Products
by All Night Media®*

CLIMBING ROSE BACKGROUND STAMP
   580K01

GREEN INK PAD 19AGR

Paper

PINK PATTERNED PAPER AG125*

GREEN PATTERNED PAPER AG138*

DIE CUT FLOWERS AG521, 3 SHEETS

Other Supplies

SHADOWBOX FRAME WITH MAT

POP DOTS™ ADHESIVE FOAM DOTS
   (ALL NIGHT MEDIA, 73DOT)

ADHESIVES OF YOUR CHOICE

Products by Anna Griffin Inc.

IRECTIONS

1. Remove glass, mat, and backing from frame.

2. Stamp Climbing Rose Background stamp on the mat with Green ink.

3. Line the inner sides of the shadow box mat with green patterned paper.

4. Cut 1/2" wide strips of pink patterned paper to line the opening of the shadowbox. Miter the corners.

5. Using foam dots, layer the die cut flowers to create a three-dimensional effect.

6. Adhere flowers inside shadowbox. Place inside frame.

GRATITUDE JOURNAL

Receiving this decorated journal would surely be something to be grateful for! Use it to write about how you are thankful for the things that have come to you.

YOU WILL NEED

Anna Griffin Products by All Night Media®

SWIRL MOTIF STAMP 580G04

SALUTATIONS STAMP SET 2483R - "WITH GRATITUDE" STAMP

PINK SATIN RIBBON 93PNK

BLACK INK PAD 19ABK

Paper

PINK FLORAL PAPER AG091*

ROSE PRINT PAPER AG085*

PINK PAPER AG015*

PINK FLORAL PAPER AG104*

PINK JOURNALING PAGE AG244*

Other Supplies

STAMP-A-MEMORY PHOTO JOURNAL, 5-1/4" X 7-1/4" (ALL NIGHT MEDIA 87SIJ)

LIGHTWEIGHT CARDBOARD

POP DOTS™ ADHESIVE FOAM DOTS (ALL NIGHT MEDIA 73DOT)

ADHESIVES OF YOUR CHOICE

Products by Anna Griffin Inc.

DIRECTIONS

1. Stamp the cover of the journal using the Swirl Motif stamp with Black ink.

2. Cut a 1" x 6-1/2" strip of pink floral paper (AG091). Adhere it on a 1-1/4" x 6-1/2" strip of rose print paper. Place it horizontally on cover, with one end next to the spiral binding, wrapping the other end to the inside. Adhere in place.

3. Cut a 4" x 5" rectangle of pink paper. Adhere on cover, using photo as a guide for placement.

4. Cut cardboard to 3-5/8" x 5". Cut 4-1/2" x 6" rectangle of rose print paper. Place cardboard in the center of paper. Fold in paper corners and adhere. Fold in each side and adhere to cardboard. Adhere on journal cover.

5. Cut flowers from both pink floral papers. Decoratively adhere the flowers to the cover with foam dots.

6. Cut a tag from the journaling page. Stamp "Gratitude" (mask the "with" on the stamp) with Black ink on the tag. Adhere to the cover with foam dots.

7. Tie a bow with pink satin ribbon. Adhere the cover.

PHOTO BOX WITH EMBOSSED FRAME

An embossed frame is a lovely addition to this paper-covered box. A very special gift can be hidden inside this beautiful box.

YOU WILL NEED

*Anna Griffin Products
by All Night Media®*

FLOURISH BRASS STENCIL 5805S

EMBOSSING TOOL 5806ST

Paper

FLORAL PAPER AG108*

GREEN PATTERNED PAPER AG043*

IVORY PAPER, 6-1/2" X 5"

Other Supplies

STAMP ART FRAME BOX (ALL NIGHT
    MEDIA 87WFB)

ROYAL COAT® DECOUPAGE FINISH
    (1401))

FOAM BRUSH

CRAFT KNIFE

2-3/4" X 4" PHOTO

ADHESIVES OF YOUR CHOICE

*Products by Anna Griffin Inc.

DIRECTIONS

1. Using a craft knife, carefully remove the frame from the box. (This will allow you to cover the frame and the box more easily.)

2. Cover the ends with green patterned paper, cutting the paper to fit the box. Adhere to the box with decoupage finish.

3. Cover the bottom of box, sides, and top of the box with floral paper. Tuck edges under carefully.

4. Cover the frame with green patterned paper. Miter the corners and tuck the ends underneath. To make the center opening, cut an "X" in the paper over the frame opening and tuck ends underneath.

5. Adhere the frame to the box on three sides, leaving one side open to insert the photo.

6. Cut out the center area of the ivory paper to make a frame 1-1/4" wide.

7. Emboss a corner design on each corner of the ivory frame, using the Embossing Tool. Center the Flourish Motif on each side and emboss.

8. Adhere the ivory embossed frame to the frame on the box.

9. Cut 1/4" wide strips of green patterned paper to frame the inner edge of the frame opening. Adhere to the embossed ivory paper, mitering the corners. Add a photo to the frame.

FOLDING FRAME

This decorated folding frame prettily holds a pair of photos. Framing the photos you send to family and friends will make them all the more special.

YOU WILL NEED

Anna Griffin Products by Plaid®

ROYAL COAT® CABBAGE ROSES DECOUPAGE PAPER (2068)

ROYAL COAT® BIRDS & FLOWERS DECOUPAGE PAPER (2069)

Paper

GREEN SOLID PAPER AG016*

Other Supplies

STAMP ART FOLDING FRAME (ALL NIGHT MEDIA 87WFF)

ROYAL COAT® DECOUPAGE FINISH (1401)

FOAM BRUSH

TEMPORARY ADHESIVE

CRAFT KNIFE

FINE STEEL WOOL

*Products by Anna Griffin Inc.

DIRECTIONS

1. Using a craft knife, carefully remove the frames from the base.

2. Measure the frame and cut a piece of green floral paper from the paper set to cover the outside of the base. Cover the base with the paper, using decoupage finish. Trim the corners diagonally before folding the edges.

3. Cut a piece of green script-patterned paper from the paper set, being careful about the direction of the pattern. Decoupage this to the inside of the base.

4. Cut two pieces of green solid paper to cover the frames. Trim the corners diagonally before folding the edges. To make the center openings, cut X-shapes from corner to corner and fold back the paper, trimming any excess.

5. Cut pink stripes from pink striped paper from paper set and apply them to the frames, mitering the corners. Use temporary adhesive while you position the pieces. Use decoupage finish to adhere.

6. Adhere the frames to the base.

7. Cut out flower bouquets from the floral paper and decoupage them to the bottom corners of the frames, allowing them to overhang slightly. Be sure they won't get in the way when the frame is standing for display.

8. To finish, apply several coats of decoupage finish to the whole project, especially to the front and back edges of the flowers that overhang the frames. Allow to dry. Lightly rub with steel wool for a smooth finish.

TULIP STAMPED BOX

This ribbon-tied box features a wrap-around cover. It's a lovely way to present a small gift.

YOU WILL NEED

*Anna Griffin Products
by All Night Media®*

ENGRAVED BACKGROUND STAMP
580K02

REPOUSSE BACKGROUND STAMP
580K06

STAMPING STARTER KIT 5809SK -
TULIP STAMP

GREEN INK PAD 19AGR

PINK INK PAD 19APK

Paper

IVORY PAPER AG113*

GREEN STRIPED PAPER AG140*

GREEN PAPER AG016*

Other Supplies

BOTTOM PART OF A PAPERBOARD
JEWELRY BOX, 3" X 3" X 1" TALL

MAT BOARD

GREEN SILK RIBBON, 1" WIDE

POP DOTS™ ADHESIVE FOAM DOTS
(ALL NIGHT MEDIA, 73DOT)

ADHESIVES OF YOUR CHOICE

Products by Anna Griffin Inc.

DIRECTIONS

1. Stamp the Repousse Background with Pink ink twice on the ivory paper. Cut out both of the stamped rectangles.

2. Adhere each stamped rectangle to a 3" square of mat board. Fold paper over the edges of the mat board. (These are the front and back covers of the box.)

3. For the spine, cut a 1" x 3" rectangle of mat board.

4. Cut a 2" x 4" rectangle from green striped paper. Lay the paper over the spine and overlap the front and back covers by about 1/2". Adhere paper in place.

5. Stamp the Engraved Background with Pink ink twice on ivory paper. Cut out both stamped rectangles. (These will line the covers.)

6. Cut two pieces of green silk ribbon, each 11" long. Sandwich a piece of ribbon between the mat board cover and the stamped Engraved Background paper. Adhere the paper to the cover.

7. Cut a 1-1/4" x 2" piece of ivory paper. Stamp the Tulip with Green ink on the paper. Rub Pink ink along the edge of the Tulip stamped rectangle.

8. Cut a 1-5/8" x 3-1/8" piece of green paper. Adhere the stamped rectangle to the green paper with foam dots and adhere to cover.

9. Glue the box bottom to the inside back cover. Tie ribbon to close box.

SPRING PLANTERS

Celebrate springtime with the gift of plants or flowers in these charming, decoupaged tin planters. Simple containers become beautiful accessories when covered with gorgeous papers.

You will need

Anna Griffin Products by Plaid®

ROYAL COAT® BIRDS & FLOWERS DECOUPAGE PAPERS (2069)

ROYAL COAT® STRAWBERRIES DECOUPAGE PAPERS (2060)

Other Supplies

2 TIN PLANTERS WITH SCALLOPED TOP EDGES, ONE 4" DIAMETER, 3" TALL; THE OTHER 5" DIAMETER, 4" TALL

ROYAL COAT® DECOUPAGE FINISH (1401)

FOAM BRUSH

GOLD SPRAY PAINT

DECORATIVE EDGE SCISSORS

FINE STEEL WOOL

Directions

Painting and Covering

1. Spray paint the tin planters with gold paint. Let dry.

2. Cut a piece of beige floral paper from the Birds & Flowers Decoupage Papers to fit the height and width of one tin planter. *Tip:* Trace the planter while rolling it across the paper for a curved piece of paper that will fit around the curved shape.

3. Cut a piece of green patterned paper from the Strawberries Decoupage Papers Set to fit the other planter.

4. Trim the upper edges of the cut papers with a pair of decorative edge scissors.

5. Apply the paper to the painted planters with decoupage finish. Let dry. Lightly buff the surfaces with steel wool.

Decorating and Finishing

1. Cut out bird and flower motifs from the Birds & Flowers Decoupage Papers. Apply cutouts to the planters with decoupage finish. Let dry.

2. Buff the entire surface of each planter with steel wool. Apply another coat of decoupage finish. Allow to dry. Fill planters with plants or flowers.

BABY TREASURE BOX & MINI FRAME

This fold-up treasure box has a frame for a photo and space for a keepsake.

OU WILL NEED

Anna Griffin Products:
by All Night Media®

FRIEZE BACKGROUND STAMP 580K04

CARRIAGE MOTIF STAMP 580E03

PURPLE INK PAD 19APR

GREEN INK PAD 19AGR

Paper

PURPLE PAPER AG033*

GREEN PAPER AG016*

Other Supplies

BABY METAL CHARM

24" LAVENDER SEAM BINDING

CHIPBOARD

TRANSPARENCY FILM

DOUBLE-SIDED TAPE

THREAD OR WIRE

ROYAL COAT® DECOUPAGE FINISH
   (1401)

FOAM BRUSH

ADHESIVES OF YOUR CHOICE

Materials for alternate colored project

ESPALIER BACKGROUND STAMP
   580K03

ANTIQUE ALPHABET STAMP SET
   2480P

GRAY INK PAD 19ASL

24" PLATINUM RIBBON

IVORY PAPER. 2 PIECES 8 1/2" X 11"

Products by Anna Griffin Inc.

IRECTIONS

Cutting the Chipboard

From chipboard, cut these pieces:

- Two 2" squares (for the base)
- Three 2" squares with 1-1/4" squares cut from the centers (for the inner box top, inner

frame, and cover frame)

- One 2" x 2" square with a 1" square cut from the center (for the mat for the cover frame)
- Four 2" x 1/4" rectangles (for the inner box sides)
- Two 2" x 1/2" rectangles (for the base sides).

Stamping

1. From green paper, cut a 1-7/8" x 5-3/8" rectangle. At one end, stamp the Carriage Motif in green ink. (This paper will line the inner box.)

2. Cut another piece of green paper 2-1/2" square to cover the square that will line the front cover frame.

3. From purple paper, cut one 3" square, two 2-1/2" squares, and one 3" x 6" rectangle. Stamp the pieces, using the Frieze Background stamp with Purple ink.

Assembly

1. Place the stamped rectangle of purple paper on your work surface, face down. Along a line about 2" from the top edge, line up pieces of chipboard in this order, leaving a 1/8" gap between the pieces: 2" square, 2" x 1/2" rectangle, 2" square, 2" x 1/2" rectangle. Adhere chipboard to paper. Trim corners on the diagonal and fold edges of paper over chipboard. (This is the cover.)

2. Cover the inside with a piece of green paper.

3. Cover the inner frame and cover frame with smaller squares of stamped purple paper, cutting an

X-shape in the open area of the frame and folding back the paper.

4. Attach three sides of the inner frame to the base with double-sided tape. (Leave one side open to insert a photo.)

5. Cover the mat of the cover frame with the smaller square of green paper. Attach the mat to the cover frame. Hang the charm from the back of the frame with wire or thread, anchoring with double-sided tape.

6. Place ribbon over the outside of the cover, centering it horizontally and allowing equal amounts of ribbon to overhang the sides.

7. Securely anchor the cover frame to the front of the cover with double-sided tape. (This also anchors the ribbon to the front and allows the ribbon to be a background for the hanging charm.)

8. Take the remaining pieces of cut chipboard and attach to the back of the remaining frame piece, making a box. Cover the box with the remaining square of purple stamped paper.

9. Attach a piece of transparency film inside the window and insert memorabilia. Glue covered box to inside of cover on left side.

To make the ivory box in the picture, use the instructions above. See materials list at left for stamps and papers.

Pictured left to right: Ivory Mini-Frame and Baby Treasure Box.

EMBOSSED DESK FRAME

An embossed paper mat, applied with ribbon corners, lends importance to a paper-covered frame.

You will need

Anna Griffin Products by All Night Media®

FLOURISH CORNER BRASS STENCIL 5805S

EMBOSSING TOOL 5806ST

FRIEZE BACKGROUND STAMP 580K04

BLUE INK PAD 19ABL

Paper

BLUE PAPER AG023*

IVORY CARD STOCK

Other Supplies

STAMP ART FRAME, 6" X 7-1/2" (ALL NIGHT MEDIA 87WFS)

ROYAL COAT® DECOUPAGE FINISH (1401)

FOAM BRUSH

GREEN RIBBON CORNERS (RC104)*

CRAFT KNIFE

ADHESIVES OF YOUR CHOICE

PHOTOGRAPH

Products by Anna Griffin Inc.

Directions

1. Cut a 7" x 8-1/2" piece of blue paper. Stamp, using the Frieze Background stamp with Blue ink.

2. Cut out the center section of the paper to make a paper frame 2" wide on all sides. Adhere to the frame with decoupage finish, matching the center opening carefully. Trim overhanging corners on the diagonal to remove excess paper. Wrap edges over the back of the frame. Let dry.

3. Use a craft knife to cut the original opening for the photo to be inserted. (This way is much cleaner and easier than keeping it open while gluing the paper.)

4. Cut a center opening in the ivory card stock to match the opening of the frame and leave a 3/4" ivory border on all sides.

5. Emboss the Flourish motif along the edges of the ivory card stock, carefully centering the motifs.

6. Attach the ivory frame to the larger frame with ribbon corners.

Half Pillow Box with Flowers

Here's an unexpected use for a pillow box – as a presentation container
for a small bouquet of fresh or dried flowers.

OU WILL NEED

*Anna Griffin Products
by All Night Media®*

SWAG CARTOUCHE STAMP 580K05

CLIMBING ROSE BACKGROUND STAMP
580K01

ANTIQUE ALPHABET STAMP SET
2480P

LAUREL MOTIF STAMP 580F03

CRIMSON INK PAD 19ABG

GREEN INK PAD 19AGR

Paper

IVORY CARD STOCK

IVORY PAPER

Other Supplies

PILLOW GIFT BOX

PINK WIRE-EDGE RIBBON

DECORATIVE EDGE SCISSORS

ROYAL COAT® DECOUPAGE FINISH
(1401)

FOAM BRUSH

HOLE PUNCH

IRECTIONS

1. Stamp the ivory paper repeatedly, using the Climbing Rose Background stamp with Green ink.

2. Cover the gift box with the stamped ivory paper, adhering with decoupage finish and being careful to score the paper at the fold lines of the box.

3. Cut off the top end of the pillow box with decorative edge scissors.

4. Fold box and glue flap.

5. Stamp the Swag Cartouche with Crimson ink on ivory card stock. Punch a hole on either side of the oval shape.

6. Cut a 2" x 4" piece of ivory card stock. Fold in half to make a small card. Stamp using the Laurel Motif stamp with Green ink. Add an initial, using an Alphabet Stamp with Crimson ink. Punch a hole in the card.

7. Wrap pillow box with ribbon and pull the ends through the holes in the Swag Cartouche and the hole in the card. Tie ribbon in a bow. Insert flowers or other gift in box.

PAPER 5 CRAFTING

for wrapping

MAKE YOUR GIFTS EVEN MORE
SPECIAL BY PACKAGING THEM
WITH BEAUTIFUL COVERINGS.
FROM BAGS AND TAGS TO
PAPER BOXES YOUR GIFTS
HAVE NEVER BEEN SO
ELEGANT.

GIFT BAGS, TAGS & TISSUE

Plain gift bags and tissue can be decorated with stamping to look anything but ordinary.

You will need

Anna Griffin Products
by All Night Media®

ROSE MOTIF STAMP 580G03

SALUTATIONS STAMP SET 2483R -
"WITH GRATITUDE" STAMP

BOUQUET MOTIF STAMP 580H01

GREEN INK PAD 19AGR

BLACK INK PAD 19ABK

Paper

GREEN TISSUE PAPER

IVORY CARD STOCK *OR* BLANK
NOTECARD

Other Supplies

BLUE GIFT BAG

DECORATIVE EDGE SCISSORS

HOLE PUNCH

VARIOUS RIBBONS, VARIOUS WIDTHS

To make a green bag, you will need
the following supplies:

ROSE MOTIF STAMP 580G03

SALUTATIONS STAMP SET 2483R - "A
VERY HAPPY BIRTHDAY" STAMP

HYDRANGEA MOTIF STAMP 580H03

GREEN INK PAD 19AGR

PINK INK PAD 19APK

CRIMSON INK PAD 19ABG

Paper

PINK TISSUE PAPER

IVORY CARD STOCK

Directions

Tissue Paper

1. While tissue paper is still folded, trim the edges with decorative edge scissors.

2. Unfold tissue. Stamp using the Motif stamp, covering the tissue.

Card

1. Cut a 4-1/2" x 6" piece of card stock. Score and fold in half.

2. Stamp the front using the Bouquet Motif stamp with Green ink. Let dry.

3. Stamp Sentiment in Black ink over the Bouquet Motif.

4. Punch a hole in the upper left corner of the card.

Assembly

1. Place gift inside gift bag and cover with tissue paper.

2. Tie card to bag handle using several ribbons tied together in a bow.

FOLDED GIFT BAG

A clever new way to use your extra scrapbook paper.

You will need

Anna Griffin Products by All Night Media®

ESPALIER BACKGROUND STAMP 580K03

SCROLL BORDER STAMP 580H08

TOPIARY MOTIF STAMP 580H05

GREETINGS STAMP SET 2484R - "JUST FOR YOU" STAMP

GOLD INK PAD 19AGL

GREEN INK PAD 19AGR

Paper

GREEN PAPER AG016*

PURPLE PATTERNED PAPER AG031*

IVORY CARD STOCK

Other Supplies

PURPLE WIRE-EDGE RIBBON, 1-1/2" WIDE

DECORATIVE EDGE SCISSORS

HOLE PUNCH

ADHESIVES OF YOUR CHOICE

Directions

The Bag

1. Cut green paper to 12" x 9-1/4". Score 1" from the top and 1-3/4" from the bottom.
2. Starting from the left side, score the paper vertically at 1/2", 2-1/4" 6-1/4", and 8".
3. Cut bottom flaps along score lines. Cut the flap off the 1/2" piece.
4. Stamp the Background stamp across what will be the front and back of the bag.
5. Stamp the Border stamp along what will be the sides.
6. Fold over the top edge and fold paper into bag shape. Fold and tuck in the 1/2" tab. Use adhesive to secure.

The Tag

1. Stamp the Motif with Gold ink on a 2-1/4" x 3-1/2" piece of ivory card stock. Let dry.
2. Stamp sentiment with Green ink over the topiary.
3. Trim the edges with the decorative edge scissors.
4. Cut a 2-1/4" x 4" piece of patterned paper. Adhere the stamped tag on the purple paper.
5. Punch a hole in the top left corner.

Assembly

1. Pinch top of bag closed and punch two holes.
2. Thread ribbon through the holes and tag. Tie in a bow.

To make a yellow bag you will need the following supplies:

Anna Griffin Products: by All Night Media®

ENGRAVED BACKGROUND STAMP 580K02

LATTICE BORDER STAMP 580H06

BOUQUET MOTIF STAMP 580H01

GOLD INK PAD 19AGL

PINK INK PAD 19APK

Paper

YELLOW PAPER AG0122*

PINK PATTERNED PAPER AG082*

IVORY CARD STOCK

Other Supplies

PINK WIRE-EDGE RIBBON, 1-1/2" WIDE

DECORATIVE EDGE SCISSORS

HOLE PUNCH

ADHESIVES OF YOUR CHOICE

Products by Anna Griffin Inc.

Directions

The Bag

1. Cut yellow paper to 12" x 9-1/4". Score 1" from the top and 1-3/4" from the bottom.
2. Starting from the left side, score the paper vertically at 1/2", 2-1/4" 6-1/4", and 8".
3. Cut bottom flaps along score lines. Cut the flap off the 1/2" piece.
4. Stamp the Engraved Background with Pink ink across what will be the front and back of the bag.
5. Stamp the Lattice Border with Pink ink along what will be the sides.
6. Fold over the top edge and fold paper into bag shape. Fold and tuck in the 1/2" tab. Use adhesive to secure.

The Tag

1. Stamp the Bouquet Motif with Gold ink on a 2-1/4" x 3-1/2" piece of ivory card stock. Let dry.
2. Trim the edges with the decorative edge scissors.
3. Cut a 2-1/4" x 4" piece of pink patterned paper. Adhere the stamped tag on the pink paper.
4. Punch a hole in the top left corner.

Assembly

1. Pinch top of bag closed and punch two holes.
2. Thread ribbon through the holes and tag. Tie in a bow.

PUNCHED GIFT TAGS

Paper punches make it easy to make these square gift tags.
To keep them in view, slide them into glassine envelopes.

You will need

To make each tag, you need a punch, patterned paper, and ivory paper. Listed below are the various supplies used to make the different tags pictured on the opposite page.

*Anna Griffin Products
by All Night Media®*

FLEUR DE LIS PUNCH 59FDL

ORNAMENTAL BRACKET PUNCH 59BRK

FLOURISH PUNCH 45FLO

Paper

IVORY PAPER

ROSE PATTERNED PAPER AG012*

BLUE PATTERNED PAPER AG117*

GREEN PATTERNED PAPER AG118*

OTHER SUPPLIES:

2-1/4" GLASSINE ENVELOPES

ADHESIVES OF YOUR CHOICE

*Products by Anna Griffin Inc.

Directions

1. Cut a 2" x 4" rectangle from patterned paper. Score and fold each in half to make a square tag.

2. Cut a 2" square from patterned paper. Adhere square to the front of the folded card.

3. Cut a 1-7/8" square of ivory paper. Decoratively punch all four corners of the square.

4. Adhere the punched square to the 2" patterned square on the card.

5. Insert card in glassine envelope.

JUST FOR YOU GIFT BOX

Special gifts need special wrappings. Use stamped paper to cover
the box and decorated paper to make a bow.

You Will Need

*Anna Griffin Products
by All Night Media®*

BOUQUET MOTIF STAMP 580H01

GREETINGS STAMP SET 2484R - "JUST
FOR YOU" STAMP

GEORGIAN CARTOUCHE STAMP
580H04

BLUE INK PAD 19ABL

GREEN INK PAD 19AGR

Paper

GREEN STRIPE PAPER AG143*

GREEN PATTERN PAPER AG003*

IVORY PAPER

Other Supplies

PAPERBOARD BOX

GREEN RIBBON

POP DOTS™ ADHESIVE FOAM DOTS
(ALL NIGHT MEDIA, 73DOT)

ADHESIVES OF YOUR CHOICE

Products by Anna Griffin Inc.

Directions

Covering the Box

1. Stamp the Bouquet Motif stamp
   on ivory paper with Blue ink.

2. Wrap box in the paper.

The Paper Ribbon and Bow

1. Cut a strip of green patterned
   paper 12" x 2".

2. Cut a strip of green striped paper
   12" x 1-3/4".

3. Center the green striped strip on
   the green patterned strip to make
   the paper ribbon.

4. Wrap green ribbon around the
   paper ribbon. Adhere to the box.

5. Cut a 2" wide strip of green
   patterned paper and a 1-3/4" wide
   strip of green striped paper. Layer
   striped paper over patterned paper
   as before. Make two loops for the
   sides of the bow. Wrap at the center
   with a narrow strip of paper. Wrap
   bow loops with green ribbon.

The Tag

1. Cut a piece of ivory paper
   2-1/2" x 2".

2. Stamp the Georgian Cartouche in
   the center with Green ink. Let dry.

3. Stamp "Just for You" in the center
   of the cartouche with Blue ink.
   Cut out the cartouche.

4. Adhere the cutout cartouche to
   the top of the paper bow with foam
   dots. Adhere bow and tag to
   the box.

Just for *You*

HAPPY BIRTHDAY BOX

Beautiful layers of flowers and a gold ribbon are artfully combined to create this festive box, which is a gift in itself. It is almost too pretty to open.

OU WILL NEED

IRECTIONS

*Anna Griffin Products
by All Night Media®*

SWIRL MOTIF STAMP 580G04

SALUTATIONS STAMP SET 2483R - "A VERY HAPPY BIRTHDAY" STAMP

GOLD INK PAD 19AGL

GOLD SATIN RIBBON 93GLD

BLACK INKPAD 19ABK

Paper

GREEN PATTERNED PAPER AG119*

FLORAL PAPER AG116*

IVORY CARD STOCK

FLORAL BORDER STICKERS AG617*

Other Supplies

ROYAL COAT® DECOUPAGE FINISH (1401)

OVAL IVORY PAPERBOARD BOX, 4-3/4" X 3-1/2", 2-1/2" TALL

POP DOTS™ ADHESIVE FOAM DOTS (ALL NIGHT MEDIA, 73DOT)

GOLD THREAD

SOFT CLOTH

ADHESIVES OF YOUR CHOICE

Products by Anna Griffin Inc.

Box Base

1. Cover the box with decorative paper using decoupage finish.

Box Lid

1. Lightly smear gold ink on the box lid.

2. Trim border sticker to fit edge of lid before removing the backing paper. Remove paper and adhere to edge of the lid.

3. Cut flowers from floral paper. Adhere on the lid with foam dots.

4. Cut a piece of ribbon to fit across lid. Fold ends under lid and adhere inside lid. Use thread to gather ribbon in the center of lid and tie.

5. Make a bow with ribbon. Adhere bow to ribbon.

Tag

1. Stamp the Swirl Motif on ivory card stock with Gold ink.

2. Cut out around the stamped image.

3. Stamp "A Very Happy Birthday" with Black ink on top of the stamped motif.

4. Attach the tag to the box underneath the ribbon.

A VERY HAPPY BIRTHDAY

HYDRANGEA PILLOW BOX

Pillow-style boxes can be decorated before assembling to make elegant, re-usable gift containers. Inking a stamp with two colors gives a custom-printed look.

 OU WILL NEED

Anna Griffin Products
by All Night Media®

HYDRANGEA MOTIF STAMP 580H03

SWAG CARTOUCHE STAMP 580K05

PURPLE INK PAD 19APR

GREEN INK PAD 19AGR

LAVENDER SATIN RIBBON 93LAV

Paper

IVORY CARD STOCK

Other Supplies

PILLOW GIFT BOX

HOLE PUNCH

POP DOTS™ ADHESIVE FOAM DOTS
    (ALL NIGHT MEDIA, 73DOT)

ADHESIVES OF YOUR CHOICE

IRECTIONS

Tag

1. Stamp the Swag Cartouche with Green ink on ivory card stock.

2. Cut out the shape. Punch a hole on either side.

Box

1. Use the pillow box as a template to cut your own box shape from ivory card stock.

2. Ink flower part of the Hydrangea stamp with Purple ink and the leaf part with Green ink. Stamp the Hydrangea randomly over the flat ivory box shape you have made. *Option:* Use the "Two Color Effects" technique explained in the Paper Crafting Techniques section.

3. Fold the box and glue to secure.

Assemble

1. Adhere the oval tag to the front of the box using a foam dot.

2. Wrap the ribbon around the box and through the holes in the tag. Tie a bow.

THREE-TIER GIFT BOXES

Create a tower of paper boxes to hold sweets for the sweet.

You will Need

Anna Griffin Products
by All Night Media®

STARTER STAMP KIT 5809SK - FLORAL
    MOTIF STAMP

CORNERS & BORDERS STAMP SET
    2482R

SALUTATIONS KIT 2483R -
    "WITH GRATITUDE" STAMP

GREEN INK PAD 19AGR

BLACK INK PAD 19ABK

Paper

GREEN PATTERNED PAPER AG118*

YELLOW PAPER AG122*

Other Supplies

GREEN WIRE-EDGE RIBBON, 1-1/2" WIDE

CRAFT KNIFE

ADHESIVES OF YOUR CHOICE

Products by Anna Griffin Inc.

Directions

Box Bottoms

1. Cut three rectangles from green patterned paper: 4" x 6", 5" x 7", and 6" x 8".

2. Score 1" from each of the long sides and 1" from each of the short sides on all three pieces. Cut the four scored lines from the short sides, creating end tabs.

3. Fold in the tabs and fold the ends of the box up and over the side tabs. Secure with adhesive.

Box Tops

1. Cut three rectangles from yellow paper: 3-7/8" x 5-7/8", 4-7/8" x 6-7/8", and 5-7/8" x 7-7/8".

2. Score 1-1/8" from each of the long sides and 1-5/8" from each of the short ends.

3. Using the score lines as guides, stamp on corners of lids using a corner stamp from the Corners & Borders set with Green ink.

4. Using the photo as a guide for placement, stamp the Floral Motif with Green ink on the box tops. (There's not room on the ends of the smallest box top.)

5. Cut, fold, and secure the tops. (See "Box Bottoms," steps 2 and 3.)

Assembly and Tag

1. Put tops and bottoms together. Tie with ribbon.

2. Cut a 1" x 3" piece of green patterned paper and 1" x 3" piece of yellow paper. Adhere the yellow paper on the green paper.

3. Stamp the yellow paper, using the Floral Motif with Green ink. Allow to dry.

4. Stamp "With Gratitude" in black ink over the motif. Adhere to top of stack.

6

for your workspace

MAKE YOUR WORKSPACE AN
EXTENSION OF YOUR CREATIVE
CAPABILITIES WITH DECORATED
BOXES THAT HOLD PAPER
AND PENS. ADD STAMPED
FILE FOLDERS, A MATCHING
CLIPBOARD AND NOTEBOOK
TO YOUR DESK TO MAKE
WORKING FUN.

ACCORDION RESUMÉ

Here's a whimsical idea for a creative person's resumé, told in story form on folded panels.

YOU WILL NEED

Anna Griffin Products
by All Night Media®

STARTER STAMP GIFT BOX 5809SK -
   TULIP MOTIF STAMP

GREETINGS STAMP SET 2484R -
   "BELIEVE" STAMP, "DREAM" STAMP

CREAM INK PAD 19ABZ

GREEN INK PAD 19AGR

Paper

PINK/BROWN FLOWERED PAPER
   AG108*, 2 SHEETS

GREEN TOILE PAPER AG119*

GREEN STRIPED PAPER AG140*

CHILDREN TOILE PAPER AG128*

PINK PATTERNED PAPER AG137*

PINK TOILE PAPER AG054*

GOLD PLUMES PAPER AG110*

LITTLE GIRL PAPER DOLL AG508*

BRIDE PAPER DOLL AG503*

FLOWER DIE CUT LC402*

ROSE DIE CUT LC401*

DIE CUT FLOWERS AG521*

IVORY CARD STOCK (SEVERAL
   SHEETS)

IVORY PAPER

Other Supplies

GOLD PHOTO CORNERS

XYRON ADHESIVE MACHINE

ADHESIVES OF YOUR CHOICE

COMPUTER AND PRINTER

*Products by Anna Griffin Inc.

DIRECTIONS

The Cover

1 Cut card stock to 12" x 6-3/4". On the left end, trim corners to create a pointed flap. On the other end, cut a 4" vertical slit 3/4" from the edge.

2. Cut one piece of pink/brown flowered paper to 12" x 6-5/8". Put through a Xyron machine face down so the glue attaches to the back of the paper. Starting at the back, attach the adhesive-coated paper to the cover. When you get to the flap, cut off the point of the card stock to match the end of the paper. Cut the slit on the back cover again through the paper.

3. Score the cover vertically from the left (pointed) side at 2", 2-1/4", 7", and 7-1/4".

The Panels

1. Cut seven pieces of ivory card stock 5-5/8" x 6-5/8". Score each one 1" from the right edge and fold.

2. Attach each panel to the next with the 1" flap, adhering the flaps to the backs of the panels. Adhere the last panel to the inside of the cover on the side with the flap.

3. Cut seven pieces of patterned paper to 4-1/4" x 6-1/4" and glue one on each inside panel.

4. Using a computer, print your resume on six 2-3/4" x 5" pieces of ivory paper. Adhere to the panels in order, using gold photo corners.

Decorating

1. Decorate each panel differently using rubber stamps and die cuts.

2. Fold resumé like an accordion. Place in cover. Secure the cover by putting the end of the flap through the cut slit on the other side.

ANNA GRIFFIN

Designer

EDUCATION

North Carolina State University

My career as a graphic designer has taken me from Atlanta to New York and back. I worked as an art director in a design firm, a marketing director for a software company and even a sales person for renowned designer Vera Wang before starting my own custom wedding invitation business in 1995.

collection of antique textiles and visual prints soon became the ... look of the company when we ... our product line to include ... Cards, Social Stationery and ... Office items in 1999. Our ... array of scrapbook products ... the craft industry in 2001. ... market we brought beautiful ... with an understated elegance ... that is our

ACCORDION ORGANIZER & NOTEPAPER HOLDER

Filing is fun and festive with this accordion organizer. Start with a plain one from an office supply store and decorate with decoupage. A pink ribbon bow holds it closed.

OU WILL NEED

Paper

FLORAL PAPER AG104*

BLUE AND GREEN PATTERNED PAPER
AG067*

PINK PATTERNED PAPER AG137*

Other Supplies

ACCORDION FILE ORGANIZER (BUY
ONE WITHOUT A COVER FLAP.)

2 PIECES CHIPBOARD, EACH THE
DIMENSIONS OF THE ACCORDION
FOLDER

1 YD. PINK WIRE-EDGE RIBBON

ROYAL COAT® DECOUPAGE FINISH
(1401)

FOAM BRUSH

CLAMPS OR BINDER CLIPS

CRAFT KNIFE

ADHESIVES OF YOUR CHOICE

Products by Anna Griffin Inc.

IRECTIONS

Making the Cover

1. Cut pieces of blue and green patterned paper 5/8" larger on all sides than the pieces of the chipboard. Adhere to the chipboard with decoupage finish. Trim the corners on the diagonal before folding over.

2. Cut two strips of pink patterned paper, each 3-3/4" wide and slightly taller than the chipboard. Attach these strips at the centers of the covered chipboard pieces.

3. Cut two strips of floral paper, each 3" wide and slightly taller than the chipboard. Attach these strips with decoupage medium to the covered chipboard pieces, using the photo as a guide for placement.

Assembly

1. Use a strong adhesive to attach chipboard pieces to the front and back of the file. Clamp securely and let dry.

2. Cut ribbon in half. Cut slits at the centers of the chipboard pieces 1-1/2" below the top edge. Slide one end of one ribbon piece down and through one slit, anchoring it about 1/2" on the reverse side of the chipboard. Repeat, using the remaining ribbon on the other cover.

3. Tie ribbon in a bow.

Make a pretty box to hold a stack of stamped note paper.

OU WILL NEED

Anna Griffin Products by All Night Media®

STARTER STAMP SET 5809SK - FLORAL
STAMP

GREEN INK PAD 19AGR

Paper

GREEN PATTERNED PAPER AG039*

FLORAL PAPER AG104*

IVORY NOTECARDS, 4" X 6"

Other Supplies

ROYAL COAT® DECOUPAGE FINISH
(1401)

FOAM BRUSH • CHIPBOARD

6" PINK WIRE-EDGE RIBBON

ADHESIVES OF YOUR CHOICE

Products by Anna Griffin Inc.

IRECTIONS

The Box

1. From the chipboard, cut these pieces:
   • one 4-1/2" x 6-1/2" (for the bottom)
   • two 1" x 6-1/2" (for the long sides)
   • two 1" x 4-1/2" (for the short sides)
   • one 1-1/2" x 4-1/2" (for the top)

2. Assemble the pieces to form a box, using the photo as a guide.

3. Cut a piece of patterned paper 10-1/2" x 7". Cover the box with the paper using decoupage finish to adhere. Tuck the ends of paper inside the box.

4. Cut piece of patterned paper 8-1/2" x 6-1/2". Adhere to inside of box using decoupage finish. Trim away excess paper to leave a smooth finish inside.

Decorating:

1. Tie a bow with the wire-edge ribbon in the center. Adhere it to top of the notepad holder.

2. Stamp bottom edges of note cards using the Floral stamp with Green ink. Place in the box.

PENCIL CUP & MINI JOURNAL

Add a decidedly feminine touch to your desk with this floral-patterned make-it-yourself pencil cup.

*Y*OU WILL NEED

Paper

FLORAL PAPER AG104*

GREEN PATTERNED PAPER AG039*

IVORY PAPER

Other Supplies

CHIPBOARD

PINK WIRE-EDGE RIBBON

ROYAL COAT® DECOUPAGE FINISH
(1401)

FOAM BRUSH

POP DOTS™ ADHESIVE FOAM DOTS
(ALL NIGHT MEDIA, 73DOT

ADHESIVES OF YOUR CHOICE

Products by Anna Griffin Inc.

*D*IRECTIONS

1. From chipboard, cut four 4"x 3" rectangles (for the sides) and one 3" square (for the bottom).

2. Assemble the cut chipboard to form a pencil cup 4" tall.

3. Cut a 5" x 12-1/2" piece of floral paper. Using decoupage medium, cover the pencil cup. Place the seam near a corner.

4. Cut an 11" square of green patterned paper. Center the pencil cup on the paper and mark the position of the base. Draw lines from each side to the edge of the paper. (You will be marking off a square at each corner.) Cut out the squares to leave a shape like a plus (+) sign. Apply decoupage medium to the back of the ivory paper and use it to line the pencil cup. Let dry.

5. Wrap the ribbon around the pencil cup. Tie a bow at the center of one side. Adhere with foam dots.

This super-easy mini journal features floral covers, a beribboned spine, and a convenient ribbon loop to hold a paper-covered pencil.

*Y*OU WILL NEED

Paper

FLORAL PAPER AG104*, 2 SHEETS

Other Supplies

MINI COMPOSITION BOOK,
3-1/4" X 4-1/2"

1/4 YD. GREEN RIBBON, 1-1/2" WIDE

ROYAL COAT® DECOUPAGE FINISH
(1401)

FOAM BRUSH

PENCIL

Products by Anna Griffin Inc.

*D*IRECTIONS

1. Cut four pieces of floral paper slightly larger than the size of the book covers.

2. Attach two pieces to the outside covers with decoupage finish, aligning the edges of the paper with the spine and allowing the paper to overlap the top, bottom, and front edges. Let dry. Trim away excess paper, using a craft knife.

3. Cut a piece of ribbon the length of the spine. Apply to the spine of the book, using decoupage finish.

4. To make the pencil loop, fold a loop of ribbon around the pencil. Position the ends of the ribbon loop against the inside back cover of the book and adhere. Remove pencil.

5. Using decoupage medium, cover the inside covers of the book with floral paper. (On the back cover, the paper covers the ribbon ends and helps hold the pencil loop.)

6. To cover the pencil, cut a strip of decorative paper the length of the pencil and about 1" wide. Apply paper to the pencil using decoupage finish. Let dry.

PANSY NOTEBOOK & PANSY CLIPBOARD

This little notebook is the perfect companion for the pansy clipboard.

OU WILL NEED

Paper

ROYAL COAT® PERFECT PANSIES
DECOUPAGE PAPER (2067)

Other Supplies

MINI COMPOSITION BOOK

ROYAL COAT® DECOUPAGE FINISH
(1401)

FOAM BRUSH

FINE STEEL WOOL

CRAFT KNIFE

Products by Anna Griffin Inc.

IRECTIONS

1. Cut two pieces of green script paper slightly larger than the covers of the book. Apply to the front and back covers of the book, using decoupage finish. Let dry. Trim away any excess paper.

2. Cut a 5" strip of purple striped paper. Apply to the spine of the book with decoupage finish. Allow to dry. Trim away excess paper.

3. Cut out pansy motifs from paper, using a craft knife. Arrange dec-

oratively on cover and glue in place with decoupage finish. Let dry.

4. Coat the cover of the book several times with decoupage finish to seal the image edges and protect the cover. Let dry between coats. Let final coat dry completely.

5. Buff surface to a smooth finish with steel wool.

Use the reverse decoupage technique to add a floral background on a clear plastic clipboard.

OU WILL NEED

Paper

ROYAL COAT® PERFECT PANSIES
DECOUPAGE PAPER (2067)

Other Supplies

ROYAL COAT® DECOUPAGE FINISH
(1401)

FOAM BRUSH

CLEAR PLASTIC CLIPBOARD

FINE STEEL WOOL

CRAFT KNIFE

DECORATIVE EDGE SCISSORS

Products by Anna Griffin Inc.

IRECTIONS

1. Cut out pansy motifs from paper. Adhere cutouts to the back of the clipboard by applying decoupage finish to the fronts of the cutouts and pressing on the back of the clipboard. (This is called "reverse decoupage.")

2. Cut two 7-1/2" strips and two 10-3/4" strips from purple striped paper. Miter the corners to form a rectangular frame. Trim the edges with decorative edge scissors.

3. Adhere the purple frame to the back of the clipboard, using the reverse decoupage technique.

4. Cut a 7-3/4" x 11" piece of green script paper. Using the reverse decoupage technique, apply to the back of the clipboard. See the photo for placement.

5. Cut a piece of yellow decoupage paper to fit the back of the clipboard. Apply it to the back of the clipboard, using the reverse decoupage technique. Allow to dry.

6. Seal the back of the clipboard with a final coat of decoupage finish. Allow to dry.

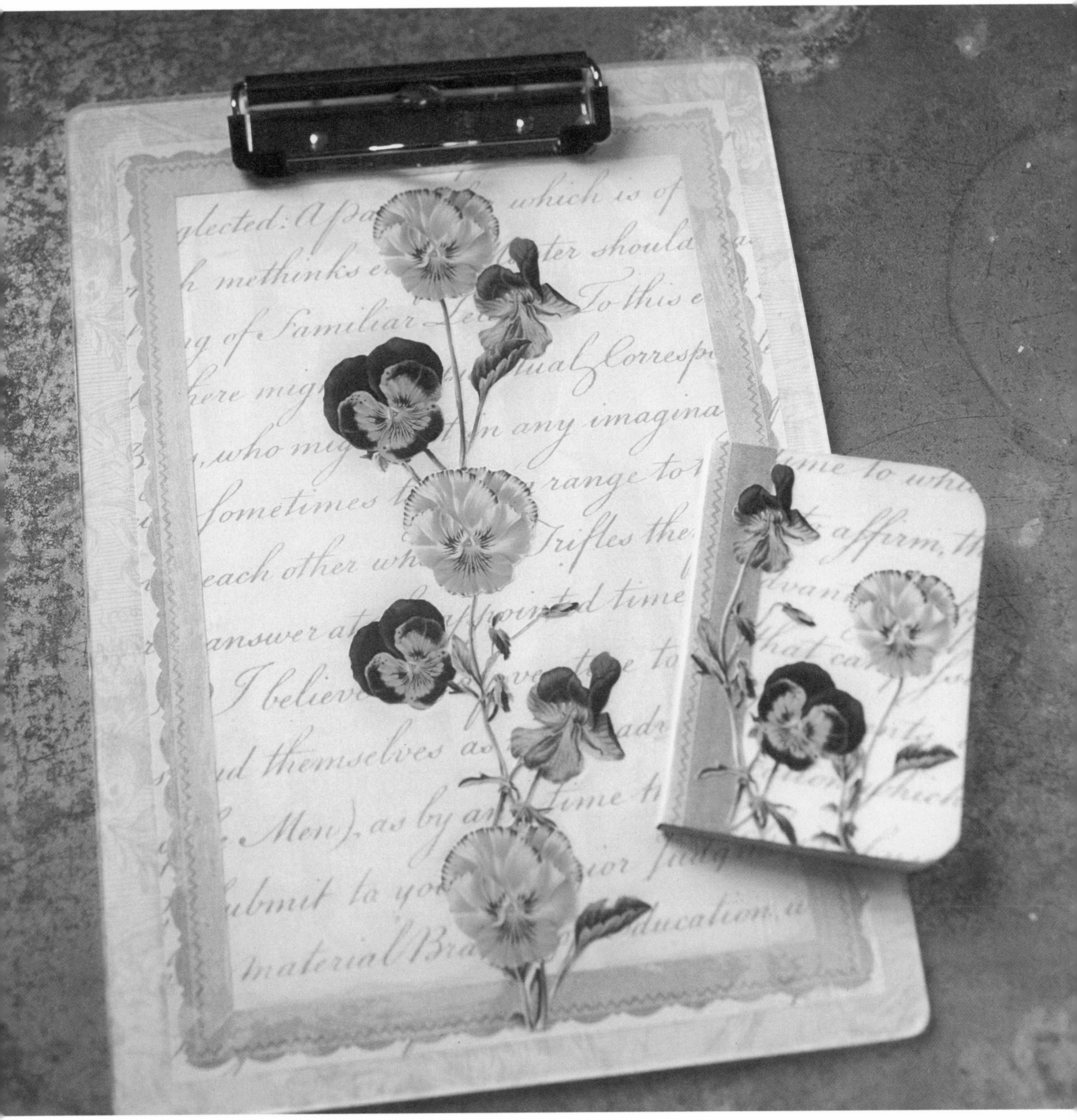

FANCY FILE FOLDERS

No more plain manila! Give your file folders personality with stamped labels
and paper linings — they will definitely make working fun.

*Y*OU WILL NEED

*Anna Griffin Products
by All Night Media®*

BASKET MOTIF STAMP 580J05

SWAG CARTOUCHE STAMP 580K05

BLUE INK PAD 19ABL

GREEN INK PAD 19AGR

Paper

BLUE STRIPED PAPER AG022*

IVORY CARD STOCK

Other Supplies

MANILA FILE FOLDERS

ROYAL COAT® DECOUPAGE FINISH
(1401)

FOAM BRUSH

COMPUTER AND PRINTER *OR* BLACK
INK PEN

*Products by Anna Griffin Inc.

*D*IRECTIONS

For each folder:

1. Adhere striped paper inside the folder on the tabbed side with decoupage medium.

2. Stamp front and back of folder, using the Basket Motif stamp with Green ink.

3. Type on a computer and print out *or* handwrite the folder title on ivory card stock.

4. Stamp the Swag Cartouche with Blue ink around the title. Cut out. Adhere to the front of the file folder.

GARDEN OF EDEN BALL

Committee Meeting

NOTES

CD ENVELOPE

Make a personalized, decorated envelope to hold a compact disc.
Give the gift of your favorite music or photographs.

You will need

*Anna Griffin Products
by All Night Media®*

RIBBON CARTOUCHE STAMP 580K08

CLIMBING ROSE BACKGROUND STAMP
   580K01

GOLD INK PAD 19AGL

PURPLE INK PAD 19APR

Paper

IVORY CARD STOCK

COLORED CARD STOCK

Other Supplies

HOOK-AND-LOOP FASTENER DOTS
   (SUCH AS VELCRO®)

COMPUTER AND PRINTER *OR* BLACK
   INK PEN

ADHESIVES OF YOUR CHOICE

Directions

The Envelope

1. Cut a piece of colored card stock to 11" x 7". Score and fold at 2-1/2" and 7-1/2" on the 11" side.

2. Stamp the Climbing Rose Background on one side with Purple ink.

3. Cut 1" off the top and 1" off the bottom up to the 7-1/2" score to make tabs. Score the tabs and fold. Adhere the tabs to the folded-over panel to create a pocket for the CD. (The first fold becomes the flap of the envelope.)

The Label

1. Type into a computer and print out *or* handwrite the label on ivory card stock.

2. Stamp the Ribbon Cartouche with Gold ink around the label.

3. Cut out the label and adhere it to the flap of the CD envelope.

The Closure

Add fastener dots to close the case.

Christening Photos
SEPTEMBER 24, 2002

Charles William Charnock

United Methodist Church
Charlotte, North Carolina

PAPER CRAFTING 7

for preserving memories

SPECIAL OCCASIONS AND
SPECIAL PHOTOGRAPHS CALL
FOR SPECIAL TREATMENT. USE
LAYERS OF PAPERS, STAMPS,
CUTOUTS, AND EMBELLISH-
MENTS TO MAKE YOUR
SCRAPBOOK PAGES SING.

NEW BABY SCRAPBOOK PAGE

Here's a lovely idea for a Mother's Day gift – great for grandma, too.

You WILL NEED

Anna Griffin Products by All Night Media®

GEORGIAN CARTOUCHE STAMP 580H04

BOTANICAL MOTIF STAMP 580E02

SCROLL BORDER STAMP 580H08

ROSE MOTIF STAMP 580G03

REPOUSSE BACKGROUND STAMP 580K06

GREEN INK PAD 19AGR

PURPLE INK PAD 19APR

Paper

GREEN PAPER AG016*

PURPLE PAPER AG033*

IVORY CARD STOCK, 2 SHEETS 12" X 12"

Other Supplies

4 PHOTOS, 3" X 3"

POP DOTS™ ADHESIVE FOAM DOTS (ALL NIGHT MEDIA, 73DOT)

ARCHIVAL-QUALITY ADHESIVES

Products by Anna Griffin Inc.

DIRECTIONS

1. Stamp the Rose Motif stamp around the edge of a 12" x 12" sheet of green paper with the Green ink.

2. Cut an 11-1/4" square of purple paper. Trim the ivory card stock to an 11" square. Adhere in layers to the green paper.

3. Stamp the Scroll Border around the edges of the ivory card stock with Green ink, leaving a 1/2" border all around. Stamp the Scroll Border with Green ink in a cross shape in the center of the ivory card stock.

4. Cut four 3-1/2" squares from the second piece of ivory card stock. Stamp them edge to edge with the Repousse Background and Purple ink.

5. Stamp the Georgian Cartouche with Green ink five times on the remaining card stock. Stamp the Botanical Motif in the center of four cartouches with Purple ink. Cut out the five cartouches.

6. Adhere the four photos to the 3-1/2" stamped squares. Mount the photo squares on the page with foam dots.

7. Using the project photo as a guide for placement, mount the Botanical cartouches around the page with foam dots.

8. Make a label with the remaining cartouche and mount in the center of the page with a foam dot.

Missy, Darren
and Little Charles

WEDDING SCRAPBOOK PAGE

Use rubber stamps designs to embellish scrapbook layouts.
Coordinate your ink colors with your favorite papers.

You will need

*Anna Griffin Products
by All Night Media®*

VICTORIAN CARTOUCHE STAMP 580J04

GREETINGS STAMP SET 2484R -
"DREAM" STAMP

REPOUSSE BACKGROUND STAMP
580K06

RIBBON BORDER STAMP 580H07

PURPLE INK PAD 19APR

IVORY RIBBON 95IVR

Paper

LAVENDER PATTERNED PAPER AG139*

LAVENDER FLORAL PAPER AG121*

LAVENDER STRIPED PAPER AG080*

2 SHEETS LAVENDER PAPER AG033*

IVORY CARD STOCK

Other Supplies

HOLE PUNCH

POP DOTS™ ADHESIVE FOAM DOTS
(ALL NIGHT MEDIA, 73DOT)

3 PHOTOS

ARCHIVAL-QUALITY ADHESIVES

Products by Anna Griffin Inc.

Directions

The Page

1. Cut one wide strip from the striped paper, including both printed ribbon stripes.

2. Stamp the Ribbon Border on lavender paper three times with Purple ink. Cut out the stamped strips. Mount on the striped paper strip with foam dots.

3. Adhere to the patterned paper 3/4" from the left side of the page.

The Top Photo Mat

1. Cut a piece of lavender paper 7-1/2" x 4-1/2" for photo mat. Stamp paper, using the Repousse Background with Purple ink.

2. Cut a 1-1/2" x 4-1/2" strip of floral paper. Adhere the strip to the back of photo mat along the left side, wrong sides together.

3. Score and fold the strip lengthwise 1/2" from left side and fold forward. Adhere the folded area in the center with a foam dot. Mount photo mat to page.

The Lower Photo Frames:

Cut two 4" x 5-5/8" rectangles from lavender paper. Stamp with the Repousse Background stamp and Purple ink. Cut out the centers, leaving frames 1/2" wide. Mount over photos with foam dots.

Decorations

1. Cut flowers from floral paper. Use them to decorate page and frames, attaching them with foam dots.

2. Stamp the Victorian Cartouche on ivory card stock with Purple ink. Stamp "Dream" in the center with Purple ink. Cut out the stamped image. Punch a hole in the top of the cutout and add ribbon. Attach cartouche to page with foam dots.

PERSONAL SCRAPBOOK PAGE

Create a portrait layout that honors someone special.

You WILL NEED

Anna Griffin Products
by All Night Media®

PLUMES MOTIF STAMP 580J06

GEORGIAN CARTOUCHE STAMP
580H04

CORNERS & BORDERS STAMP SET
2482R - CORNER LATTICE STAMP

BLACK INK PAD 19ABK

GOLD SATIN RIBBON 95GLD

Paper

GREEN STRIPED PAPER AG053*

BLACK PATTERNED PAPER AG034*

BROWN PAPER AG029*

BROWN PATTERNED PAPER AG110*

BLACK DIE CUT FRAME AG248*

IVORY CARD STOCK

2 SHEETS BLACK CARD STOCK

Other Supplies

STAMP-A-MEMORY ARCHIVAL DYE INK
PAD - SOFT WHEAT (ALL NIGHT
MEDIA #22SWH)

CREAM GIFT TAG (ALL NIGHT MEDIA
#80MMA)

4 BLACK BUTTONS

TAN CHALK

POP DOTS™ ADHESIVE FOAM DOTS
(ALL NIGHT MEDIA, 73DOT)

BLACK AND WHITE PHOTO

ARCHIVAL-QUALITY ADHESIVES

Products by Anna Griffin Inc.

DIRECTIONS

The Page

1. Cut a 9-1/2" square of black card stock. Center and adhere to black toile paper.

2. Cut a 9" square of black patterned paper. Center and adhere to page.

3. Cut four narrow strips from green striped paper. Place along the four sides of the black card stock to form a border. Adhere a black button where the strips intersect.

Photo Frame and Mats

1. Punch out a die cut frame. Stamp on reverse side using Plumes stamp with Soft Wheat ink. Place on photo.

2. Mount on black card stock and trim, leaving a narrow border. Place on brown patterned paper, then brown paper, then black card stock, trimming each time and leaving a border.

3. For bottom mat, stamp Plumes Motif with Black ink on brown paper. Cut mat for photo.

4. Stamp Corner Lattice on brown paper with Black ink. Cut out corners around stamped images. Mount on frame with foam dots.

The Tag

1. Rub tag with tan chalk to make it look old.

2. Stamp Plumes Motif with Black ink on the tag.

3. Stamp the Georgian Cartouche with Black ink on ivory card stock. Cut around stamped image. Add black button and journaling. Mount on tag with foam squares. Add ribbon to tag. Place tag on page.

David
1958

HERITAGE SCRAPBOOK PAGE

Layered cutouts provide dimension, and the soft colors don't overpower the vintage photo. A stamped letter acts as a monogram.

You WILL NEED

Anna Griffin Products by All Night Media®

GEORGIAN CARTOUCHE STAMP 580H04

ESPALIER BACKGROUND STAMP 580K03

FILIGREE ALPHABET STAMP SET 2485P

MEDALLION MOTIF STAMP 580J02

GRAY INK PAD 19ASL

Paper

IVORY PATTERNED PAPER AG011*

IVORY FLORAL PAPER AG071*

IVORY PAPER AG009*

PLATINUM STRIPED PAPER AG090*

CREAM FLORAL PAPER AG070*

FRAME PAGE - CREAM AG709*

FLORAL STICKERS AG618*

Other Supplies

IVORY SATIN BOW

STAMP-A-MEMORY ARCHIVAL DYE INK PAD - SOFT WHEAT (ALL NIGHT MEDIA #22SWH)

POP DOTS™ ADHESIVE FOAM DOTS (ALL NIGHT MEDIA, 73DOT)

VINTAGE PHOTOGRAPH

ARCHIVAL-QUALITY ADHESIVES

Products by Anna Griffin Inc.

DIRECTIONS

1. Cut a 10-1/2" square from cream floral paper. Adhere to center of ivory patterned paper.

2. Cut a 10-1/2" square from ivory floral paper. Adhere to center of cream floral paper.

3. Cut narrow strips of platinum striped paper. Place three narrow ribbon stripes on ivory floral paper vertically centering the middle stripe on page. Evenly space the remaining strips across the page. Adhere only on the ends. Place horizontal strips on page, weaving them over and under the vertical strips to create a lattice design.

4. Cut wider strips from platinum striped paper. Use them to make a frame around the ivory floral paper, mitering the corners.

5. Cut around clear edges of stickers. Place floral stickers around photo. Adhere to page with foam dots.

The Tag

1. Stamp the Medallion Motif on ivory paper with Soft Wheat ink. Then stamp the Espalier Background with Gray ink.

2. Cut a 3-1/2" x 4-1/2" rectangle from the stamped paper. Mount in a cream frame.

3. Cut 2" x 3" from the stamped paper and adhere onto the frame.

4. Stamp the Georgian Cartouche on ivory paper with Gray ink. Stamp a Filigree Initial inside the cartouche with Gray ink. Cut out the cartouche. Adhere to the tag with foam dots. Add the satin bow.

WEDDING ALBUM COVER

A stamped cartouche and floral cutouts personalize an six-ring binder-style album with a floral-printed cover.

YOU WILL NEED

*Anna Griffin Products
by All Night Media®*

SWAG CARTOUCHE STAMP 580K05

GREEN INK PAD 19AGR

Paper

PINK AND YELLOW FLORAL PAPER
AG017*

PINK STRIPED PAPER AG086*

YELLOW PAPER AG122*

IVORY CARD STOCK

Other Supplies

SCRAPBOOK ALBUM, 7-1/2" SQUARE
WITH A 3-RING BINDER (BB005)*

COMPUTER AND PRINTER *OR* BLACK
INK PEN

POP DOTS™ ADHESIVE FOAM DOTS
(ALL NIGHT MEDIA, 73DOT)

ARCHIVAL-QUALITY ADHESIVES

Products by Anna Griffin Inc.

DIRECTIONS

1. Cut out flower motifs from the floral paper.

2. Stamp the Swag Cartouche on ivory card stock with Green ink. Inside the cartouche, handwrite or print from a computer the title of the album. Cut out cartouche along oval shape.

3. Remove the ribbon from the scrapbook. This will be used later.

4. Cut a 6" square of yellow paper. Adhere the yellow square to the center of the scrapbook cover.

5. Cut stripes from pink striped paper. Adhere these strips around the edges of the yellow square to make a frame, mitering the corners.

6. Adhere the cut flowers to the yellow paper using foam dots.

7. Adhere the stamped title cartouche in the center.

8. Make a bow from the scrapbook ribbon and attach at the bottom of the title cartouche.

The
May · Schuh
Wedding
June 17th
1975

WEDDING ALBUM PAGES

Each of these pages is a beautiful layered memory collage designed to fit the album's slip-in sleeves. Quadrant paper, cut in four squares, supplies the background for each page.

You will need

Anna Griffin Products by All Night Media®

REPOUSSE BACKGROUND STAMP 580K06

Paper

YELLOW AND GREEN QUADRANT PAPER AG130*

PINK AND YELLOW FLORAL PAPER AG017*

GREEN STRIPED PAPER AG004*

YELLOW SCRIPT PAPER AG037*

GREEN PATTERNED PAPER AG138*

YELLOW PAPER AG122*

GREEN LOWERCASE SCRIPT ALPHABET STICKERS AG610*

Other Supplies

FLORAL SCRAPBOOK (SB005)*

VERSAMARK WATERMARK INK PAD (ALL NIGHT MEDIA 33WTR)

POT DOTS™ ADHESIVE FOAM DOTS (ALL NIGHT MEDIA, 73DOT)

ASSORTED PEARL BUTTONS

4 PHOTOS

ARCHIVAL QUALITY ADHESIVES

Products by Anna Griffin Inc.

Directions

Yellow Framed Page

1. Cut a 5-7/8" square of yellow paper. Use the Versamark pad to stamp the Repousse Background on the paper.

2. Cut a 4" square from center of paper. Reserve the square for the Flower Page.

3. Cut four 1/2" x 4-1/2" strips from green patterned paper (AG118). Adhere 1/2" under each inner edge of the frame to make a "mat."

4. Cut a 6" square of green patterned paper (AG138). Adhere frame to square.

5. Cut two 1/2" x 5-7/8" strips of green patterned paper (AG118). Adhere along center of two sides of frame. Adhere button where strips cross.

6. Place photo on yellow paper. Cut out two pink flowers from edge of floral paper. Adhere flowers along inside edge of frame. Tuck photo behind the leaves and adhere leaves with foam dots.

The
May Schuh
Wedding
June 17th

IRECTIONS

Flower Page

1. Adhere reserved yellow square from Yellow Framed Page on a 4-1/2" square of green patterned paper (AG118).

2. Adhere on yellow floral square from quadrant paper. Adhere on 6" square of yellow paper. Adhere photo on yellow paper.

3. Cut out whole pink flower from floral paper. Adhere flower on page with photo, using foam dots behind leaves.

Love Page

1. Cut a 5-7/8" square of yellow script paper. Adhere on a 6" square of green patterned paper.

2. Cut a 1-1/8" x 12" strip from green striped paper. Cut a 1/2" x 12" strip of green patterned paper. Adhere at the center of the green striped strip. Cut in two pieces, each 5-7/8" long. Adhere 1/2" from top and right sides of paper. Add a pearl button where the strips cross.

3. Adhere photo on yellow paper. Cut a pink flower from corner of floral paper. Adhere flower on page with photo, using foam dots behind leaves.

4. Place letter stickers on page to spell "love."

Flower-edged Page

1. Adhere yellow floral square from quadrant paper on 6" square of green patterned paper (AG118).

2. Place photo on yellow paper.

3. Cut pink flowers from edges of floral paper. Adhere flowers on page with photo, using foam dots behind photo.

8

PAPER CRAFTING

for entertaining

THERE ARE NUMEROUS WAYS
TO USE YOUR PAPER CRAFTING
SKILLS TO ENTERTAIN WITH
STYLE. MAKE BEAUTIFUL
INVITATIONS, PLACE CARDS,
GUEST BOOKS, AND EVEN A
MENU EASEL.

Revive the tradition of afternoon tea with this lovely invitation. A stitched pocket and antique buckle make a charming statement.

 OU WILL NEED

 IRECTIONS

*Anna Griffin Products
by All Night Media®*

BLOSSOM MOTIF STAMP 580D07

CRIMSON INK PAD 19ABG

Paper

RED PAPER AG028*

PINK PAPER AG015*

FLORAL PAPER AG024*

IVORY CARD STOCK

Other Supplies

PINK WIRE-EDGE RIBBON,
  1-1/2" w X 12" LONG

IVORY ORGANDY RIBBON, 2" WIDE

SEWING MACHINE

HAND SEWING NEEDLE

RED SEWING THREAD

VINTAGE MOTHER OF PEARL BELT
  BUCKLE

COMPUTER AND PRINTER *OR* BLACK
  INK PEN

HOLE PUNCH, 3/16"

Products by Anna Griffin Inc.

The Pocket

1. Cut a 4-1/2" x 6-1/2" rectangle from floral paper.
2. Measure 1-1/8" from the bottom edge and 7/8" from the left side. Lightly mark this spot with a pencil.
3. Measure 1-1/8" from the bottom edge and 7/8" from the right side. Lightly mark this spot with a pencil.
4. Connect the two marks lightly with a pencil and straight edge. The line should measure 2-3/4".
5. Measure 3-1/8" up from the bottom edge and 7/8" from the right side. Mark. Lightly draw a vertical line from the new mark to the horizontal line.
6. Measure 3-1/8" up from the bottom edge and 7/8" from the left side. Mark. Lightly draw a vertical line from the new mark to the horizontal line.(This is the sewing guide for the pocket.)
7. Cut a 3" piece of ivory organdy ribbon. Place the piece of ribbon over the sewing guide. Be sure the guide can be seen through the ribbon and that the ribbon overlaps each line by about 1/8".
8. Starting at the top right, stitch, using a sewing machine, over the penciled guide with red thread. Cut the thread.
9. With a sewing needle, pull the ends of the threads to the back of the paper. Tie off the threads and trim.

The Announcement Card

1. On the computer, make a rectangle 2-5/8" x 3-3/4". Place the announcement text in the bottom 2" of the rectangle, leaving the top 1-3/4" blank. Print the announcement on ivory card stock. Cut out. *Option:* Write the announcement on a 2-5/8" x 3-3/4" piece of ivory card stock.
2. Stamp the Blossom Motif with Crimson ink at the top center of the card. Allow to dry. Place the card in the pocket.

Assembly

1. Cut a 5-1/4" x 7-1/4" rectangle from red paper.
2. Cut a 5" x 7" pink paper rectangle.
3. On the rectangle with the pocket, measure down 1/4" from the top. Find the horizontal center and mark it. Measure 3/16" to the left and right of the center and mark with dots. Mark again with dots 7/16" from the center. (These dots are the guides for the punched holes.)
4. Layer the three rectangles as shown.
5. Using the hole punch, punch four holes over the marked dots.
6. Working from front to back, thread the pink ribbon through either side of the buckle and through the two interior center holes. Pull tight so that the buckle rests securely on top of the announcement. Take the left side of the ribbon and thread it up through the remaining left hole. Repeat this on the right side. Pull the ribbon tight so that there is no slack left on the back side. Trim the ends of the ribbon.

Please join us for

Afternoon Tea

to celebrate the 50th Birthday of

Eloise Sanders

Thursday, the seventh of August

at four o'clock

Bimini Bay Café

West Palm Beach

REHEARSAL DINNER INVITATION

A simple motif stamp creates an elegant background for an invitation wrapped in a vellum sleeve.

YOU WILL NEED

*Anna Griffin Products
by All Night Media®*

MEDALLION MOTIF STAMP 580J02

BLUE INK PAD 19ABL

Paper

BLUE PAPER AG023*

IVORY CARD STOCK

VELLUM

Other Supplies

DECORATIVE EDGE SCISSORS

COMPUTER AND PRINTER

ADHESIVES OF YOUR CHOICE

Products by Anna Griffin Inc.

DIRECTIONS

Invitation

1. Cut a piece of blue paper 4-1/4" x 6-1/4." Stamp the Medallion Motif with Blue ink in the center.

2. Type the text of the invitation into the computer and print out on the blue paper.

3. Cut a piece of ivory card stock to 4-3/4" x 7." Adhere the invitation on the card stock.

Vellum Sleeve

1. Cut a piece of vellum 7" x 8". Score 1" in from the left, right, and bottom edges. Cut out 1" square" on the bottom left and right corners. Fold on scored lines.

2. Fold bottom section up to become the back of the vellum sleeve. Adhere to the 1" flaps on either side.

3. Cut along the top with decorative edge scissors. Insert invitation into sleeve.

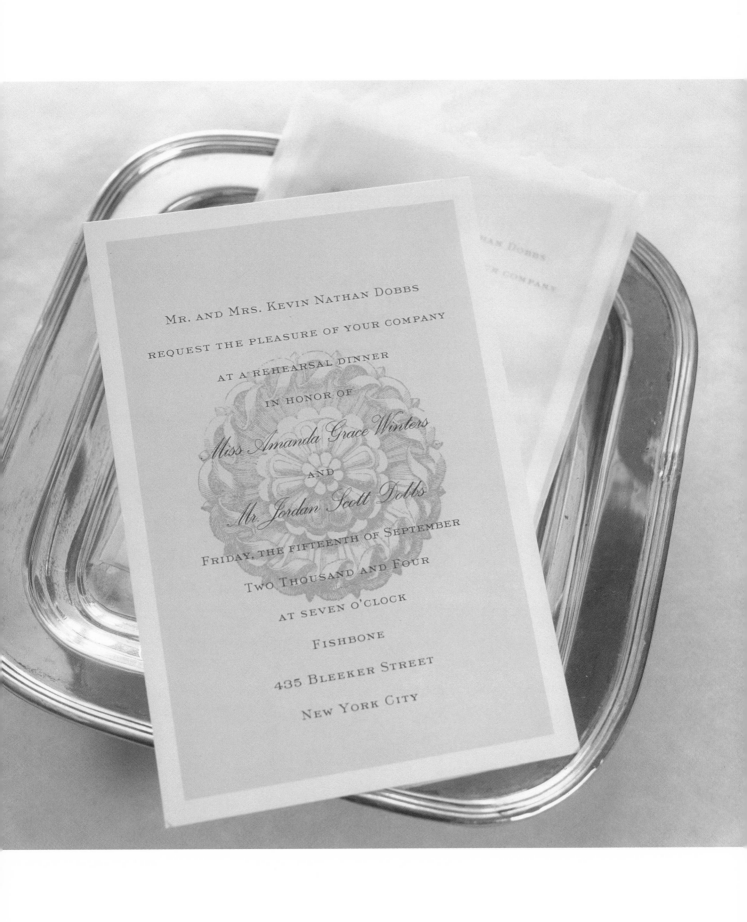

MR. AND MRS. KEVIN NATHAN DOBBS

REQUEST THE PLEASURE OF YOUR COMPANY

AT A REHEARSAL DINNER

IN HONOR OF

Miss Amanda Grace Winters

AND

Mr. Jordan Scott Dobbs

FRIDAY, THE FIFTEENTH OF SEPTEMBER

TWO THOUSAND AND FOUR

AT SEVEN O'CLOCK

FISHBONE

435 BLEEKER STREET

NEW YORK CITY

WEDDING INVITATION

Subtle yet elegant details like embossing and watermark inks
create a one-of-a-kind card for a special occasion.

You will need

*Anna Griffin Products
by All Night Media®*

SCROLL BORDER STAMP 580H08

CLIMBING ROSE BACKGROUND STAMP
  580K01

CREAM INK PAD 19ABZ

IVORY SATIN RIBBON 95IVR

Paper

CREAM PAPER AG009*

IVORY CARD STOCK, 2 SHEETS

IVORY ENVELOPE A7, 7-1/4" X 5-1/4"

Other Supplies

PEARL EMBOSSING POWDER

HEAT IT CRAFT TOOL (ALL NIGHT
  MEDIA 37HET)

DECORATIVE EDGE SCISSORS

ADHESIVES OF YOUR CHOICE

*Products by Anna Griffin Inc.

Directions

Card

1. Cut ivory card stock to 10" x 7". Score and fold in half.

2. Stamp Climbing Rose Background on cream paper with cream ink, covering a 6-3/4" x 4-3/4" area. Cut out this area. Adhere to the front of the card.

3. Stamp a 10" strip of ivory card stock using the Scroll Border stamp with Cream ink.

4. Shake pearl embossing powder on the stamped Scroll Border. Heat to emboss.

5. Cut out the embossed strip with decorative edge scissors, leaving a 1/4" border on either side. Color the edges of the strip with the Cream ink.

6. Wrap the embossed strip around the card and adhere ends together in the back. Wrap with ribbon and tie a bow.

Envelope Liner

1. Stamp the Climbing Rose on cream paper with cream ink.

2. Trim to fit the envelope. Adhere liner inside envelope.

SEASHELL PLACE CARDS

A collage of sea shells, ink, paper, and ribbon make perfect summertime place cards.

 OU WILL NEED

 IRECTIONS

*Anna Griffin Products
by All Night Media®*

ESPALIER BACKGROUND STAMP
580K03

ENGRAVED BACKGROUND STAMP
580K02

CREAM INK PAD 19ABZ

BLUE INK PAD 19ABL

GOLD SATIN RIBBON 95GLD

Paper

BLUE PAPER AG023*

IVORY CARD STOCK

Other Supplies

SMALL SEASHELLS

POP DOTS™ ADHESIVE FOAM DOTS
(ALL NIGHT MEDIA, 73DOT)

BLACK INK PEN

HOLE PUNCH

ADHESIVES OF YOUR CHOICE

Products by Anna Griffin Inc.

1. Cut an 8" x 3" piece of ivory card stock. Fold in half. Stamp using the Engraved Background with Cream ink.

2. Cut a 2-3/4" x 3-3/4" piece of blue paper. Stamp using the Espalier Background with Blue ink.

3. Cut out a 1-3/4" square (centered left and right) and 1/2" from the top edge from the blue stamped piece.

4. Cut out a 1-1/2" square from the front panel of the stamped ivory card stock, centered left to right and 5/8" from the top fold.

5. Cut a 2" x 3/4" piece of ivory card stock and 1-3/4" x 1/2" piece of blue paper. Write a name on the blue paper. Adhere with foam dots on ivory card stock. Adhere to stamped blue paper as shown.

6. Hold the stamped blue paper and ivory card together and punch a hole through both layers underneath the name, halfway between the name and the bottom of the card.

7. Pull 6" of ribbon through the hole of the blue layer. Wrap around the card under the blue paper. Secure ribbon and blue stamped paper to card. Wrap the end of the ribbon around the card, pulling the free end through the punched hole. Tie a bow and trim ends.

8. Attach a seashell to the ribbon in the cutout square with glue or a foam dot.

BEAUTIFUL VOTIVE CANDLES

Use punches, embossing stencils, and stamps to create simple,
elegant coverings for ordinary round glass votives.

OU WILL NEED

Anna Griffin Products
by All Night Media®

FLOURISH PUNCH 45FLO

SILVER SATIN RIBBON 93SLV

Paper

2 SHEETS VELLUM, 8-1/2 X 11"

Other Supplies

ROUND GLASS VOTIVE

ADHESIVE

DIRECTIONS

1. Cut two 7" x 2-5/8" pieces of vellum.

2. Punch one piece along one long side, starting in the center of the sheet with the vellum positioned as far into the punch as it will go. Punch to the end of the piece, overlapping the punches slightly, and then punch to the other end.

3. Punch the other long side,

matching the top of each punch with one on the other side.

4. With a little bit of adhesive, attach the punched vellum to the other piece. Wrap both around the glass votive and adhere.

5. Wrap a piece of platinum ribbon around the base of the votive and adhere to the vellum.

Emboss vellum to wrap around a glass votive holder.

OU WILL NEED

Anna Griffin Products
by All Night Media®

DAMASK BRASS STENCIL 5800S

EMBOSSING TOOL 5806ST

Paper

VELLUM

DIRECTIONS

1. Cut a 7" x 3" piece of vellum.

2. Emboss the vellum, using the Damask embossing template and embossing tool. Start in the middle of the paper to give a

balanced repeat of the image around the candle.

3. Wrap the vellum around the glass votive holder and adhere the ends in place.

Stamp a piece of vellum to wrap a votive holder.

OU WILL NEED

Anna Griffin Products
by All Night Media®

REPOUSSE BACKGROUND STAMP
    580K06

SILVER SATIN RIBBON 93SLV

Paper

VELLUM

DIRECTIONS

1. Cut a 3" x 7" piece of vellum.

2. Stamp the Repousse Background on the vellum with white ink, covering the vellum with the design. Allow to dry.

3. Trim the top edge of the vellum

with decorative edge scissors.

4. Wrap the vellum around the glass votive and adhere in place.

5. Wrap silver ribbon around votive. Tuck ends under edge of vellum to the cover.

Pictured left to right: Punched Votive, Embossed Votive, and Stamped Votive.

EMBOSSED GUEST BOOK

Use a guest book to record the names of guests for receptions,
dinner parties, and other memorable occasions.

YOU WILL NEED

*Anna Griffin Products
by All Night Media®*

FRENCH SWAG LARGE BRASS STENCIL
   5802S

CLIMBING FLOURISH CORNER BRASS
   STENCIL 5804S

EMBOSSING TOOL 5806ST

PINK INK PAD 19APK

Paper

FLORAL PAPER AG124*, 2 SHEETS

PINK PATTERNED PAPER AG087*, 2
   SHEETS

IVORY CARD STOCK

PAPER FOR THE PAGES

Other Supplies

CHIPBOARD

PINK SILK RIBBON

DRILL

ROYAL COAT® DECOUPAGE FINISH
   (1401)

FOAM BRUSH

COMPUTER AND PRINTER, OR BLACK
   INK PEN

ADHESIVES OF YOUR CHOICE

Products by Anna Griffin Inc.

DIRECTIONS

Making the Cover

1. Cut four pieces of chipboard, two 8" x 3/4" (for the front and back binding) and two 8" x 10-1/2" (for the covers).

2. Cut two sheets of floral paper 9" x 12". Cut ivory card stock to 10-1/8" x 7-1/2".

3. Place one binding piece and one cover piece of chipboard on each sheet of floral paper, arranging them according to Fig. 1, with 1/2" in from the long edges and 1/4" in from the short edges, leaving a 1/8" gap between the pieces. Adhere the chipboard to the paper with decoupage medium. Cut corners on the diagonal and fold the edges of the paper to the inside. Adhere.

4. Cut two pieces of pink patterned paper, each 7-7/8" x 11-1/4". Adhere these to the inside covers, pressing the paper firmly into the gap between the chipboard pieces.

Embossing

1. On ivory card stock, emboss the Climbing Flourish Corner in each corner. *Tip:* Use a light box for accurate placement.

2. Emboss French Swags on sides between corner embossing. Allow the edges of the designs to overlap slightly between repeats to create one continuous swag. See the photo for placement.

3. Attach the embossed sheet to the front cover.

Binding

1. Drill seven holes along the left edge of the front cover and the right edge of the back cover, lining up the holes.

2. Cut the paper for the pages and drill to match the covers.

3. Assemble book and bind with pink ribbon.

Title

1. Type the title into a computer and print out on ivory card stock. (You want it to fit the center area of the front cover.) *Option:* Write with ink on ivory card stock.

2. Cut out title. Edge with Pink ink. Adhere to front cover.

Elizabeth and Johnathon
JUNE 14, 2003

TULIP PLACE CARDS

These charming stamped place cards are a lovely addition to
your table decorations for a luncheon or special dinner.

YOU WILL NEED

*Anna Griffin Products
by All Night Media®*

TULIP MOTIF STAMP 580J07

REPOUSSE BACKGROUND STAMP
580K06

GREEN INK PAD 19AGR

PINK INK PAD 19APK

GREEN SATIN RIBBON 93GRN

Paper

GREEN PAPER AG016*

IVORY CARD STOCK

Other Supplies

POP DOTS™ ADHESIVE FOAM DOTS
(ALL NIGHT MEDIA, 73DOT)

HOLE PUNCH

DECORATIVE EDGE SCISSORS

COMPUTER AND PRINTER *OR* BLACK
INK PEN

Products by Anna Griffin Inc.

DIRECTIONS

For each place card:

1. Cut a 3-1/4" x 6-1/2" rectangle
   from green paper. Score and fold
   in half.

2. Stamp with the Repousse
   Background and Green ink.

3. From the ivory card stock, cut a
   3" square.

4. Stamp the card stock with the
   Tulip Motif, using Pink ink on the
   flower and Green ink on the leaves
   and stem. Trim the square with
   decorative edge scissors.

4. Type name in computer and print
   out on card stock. *Option:* Write
   name with black ink.

5. Cut out into small rectangle with
   the name and edge with Pink ink.
   Punch a hole in the left end and
   thread ribbon through. Tie in
   a knot.

6. Adhere name tag to the place card
   with foam dots.

BABY SHOWER INVITATION

Make a special invitation worthy of a new arrival!

 **Y**OU WILL NEED

*Anna Griffin Products
by All Night Media®*

CORNERS & BORDERS STAMP SET
   2482R - SWAG BORDER STAMP

ESPALIER BACKGROUND STAMP
   580K03

ANTIQUE ALPHABET STAMP SET
   2485P

GOLD INK PAD 19AGL

BLUE INK PAD 19ABL

Paper

BLUE PAPER AG023*, 2 SHEETS

GREEN PAPER AG016*

IVORY CARD STOCK, 2 SHEETS
   8-1/2" X 11"

Other Supplies

DECORATIVE EDGE SCISSORS

COMPUTER AND PRINTER *OR* BLACK
   INK PEN

ADHESIVES OF YOUR CHOICE

Products by Anna Griffin Inc.

DIRECTIONS

1. Construct a piece of card stock 16" x 3-1/4". (You will need to piece it together.) Cover with blue paper. Score every 3-1/4" and fold, accordion style.

2. Cut four 3" squares of ivory card stock. Type in a computer and print out *or* handwrite the shower invitation on card stock. Cut out to make a fifth 3" square.

3. Stamp a 4" x 4" area of blue paper with the Espalier Background and Blue ink. Cut four 1-3/4" squares from the stamped blue paper. Trim edges with decorative edge scissors.

4. Cut four 1-1/4" squares of green paper. Stamp the green squares

with Antique Alphabet letters and Gold ink to spell out "BABY" (one letter per square). Adhere each green stamped square to a blue stamped square.

5. Stamp the four edges of the blank ivory card stock squares with the Swag Border. Stamp the top edge of the fifth square (the one with the invitation printed on it).

6. Adhere one of the blue and green B-A-B-Y squares to each stamped bordered ivory square.

7. Adhere ivory squares to the panels of the blue accordion-folded piece, placing the invitation on the last panel.

SHOWER!
for Anne Bishop
SATURDAY, APRIL 16TH
AT ONE O'CLOCK
134 LAKEVIEW DRIVE
ATLANTA
R.S.V.P. 404-234-4354

SHOWER!
for Anne Bishop
SATURDAY, APRIL 16TH
AT ONE O'CLOCK
134 LAKEVIEW DRIVE
ATLANTA
R.S.V.P. 404-234-4354

BIRTHDAY PARTY INVITATION

A festive invitation sets the stage for celebrating another year.

 **You will need**

*Anna Griffin Products
by All Night Media®*

RIBBON BORDER STAMP 580H07

EMPIRE BORDER STAMP 580H10

PURPLE INK PAD 19APR

GREEN INK PAD 19AGR

Paper

IVORY CARD STOCK

Other Supplies

PURPLE WIRE-EDGE RIBBON,
    1-1/2" WIDE

POP DOTS™ ADHESIVE FOAM DOTS
    (ALL NIGHT MEDIA, 73DOT)

COMPUTER AND PRINTER

HOLE PUNCH

 **Directions**

To make one invitation:

1. Cut ivory card stock to 7-1/4" x 5-1/4" for the background piece.

2. Type invitation text into a computer and print out on ivory card stock. Trim to 4-1/2" x 6-1/4".

3. Stamp the invitation piece with the Empire Border and Purple ink around all four sides.

4. Stamp the background piece with the Ribbon Border across the top and bottom with Green ink.

5. Punch a hole at each side of the invitation card.

6. Thread ribbon through the holes and tie each end in a knot.

7. Adhere the invitation to the background with foam dots.

PLEASE COME TO MY
Birthday Party
SATURDAY, JUNE 8TH
AT ONE O'CLOCK
874 WILLOW LANE
ATLANTA

JOSH JACOBS

Decoupage Menu and Easel

This reusable easel displays the menu for a dinner party or luncheon.
After the party, save the menu for your album.

You will need

Paper

ROYAL COAT™ APPLES & PEARS
   DECOUPAGE PAPERS (2076)

IVORY PAPER

Other Supplies

ROYAL COAT® DECOUPAGE FINISH
   (1401)

FOAM BRUSH

CHIPBOARD

2 SMALL MAGNETS

CRAFT GLUE

COMPUTER AND PRINTER

FINE STEEL WOOL

POP DOTS™ ADHESIVE FOAM DOTS
   (ALL NIGHT MEDIA, 73DOT)

Directions

1. Cut a piece of chipboard 6-1/2" x 7-3/4". Cut a second piece 4-1/2" x 6".

2. Type your menu into a computer and print out on ivory paper. Trim to 3-3/4" x 5-3/4".

3. Cover the larger piece of chipboard with apples and pears paper, using decoupage finish to adhere the paper. Let dry. Coat entire surface with decoupage finish. Let dry. Buff with steel wool. Apply a second coat of decoupage finish. Let dry.

4. Cover the smaller piece of chipboard with green striped paper, using decoupage finish to adhere the paper. Let dry. Coat entire surface with decoupage finish. Let dry. Buff with steel wool. Apply a second coat of decoupage finish. Let dry.

5. Adhere the green striped piece to the apple and pear piece with foam dots.

6. Create an easel back by cutting a 4" x 6-1/4" piece of chipboard, folding it in half, and covering it with green striped paper. Adhere to the back of the other pieces with craft glue. Let dry.

7. Cut out a small green apple. Coat the front with decoupage finish and allow to dry. Adhere one of the magnets to the back of the apple cutout with craft glue.

8. Adhere the second magnet to the top of the easel. Slide the menu between the magnets.

MENU

MIXED FIELD GREENS,
ROASTED PEPPERS, AND TOMATOES
WITH BALSAMIC VINAIGRETTE

·

BAKED HADDOCK
WITH SEAFOOD STUFFING

·

CHICKEN INTERNATIONAL
WITH PARMESAN CHEESE,
GARLIC, AND GREEN ONION

·

GARLIC AND HERB
MASHED POTATOES

·

SEASONAL VEGETABLE BUNDLE
WRAPPED IN A RING OF SUMMER SQUASH

·

GOURMET ROLLS
AND SWEET BUTTER

·

HOMEMADE POUND CAKE

Glossary

A

Accordion Fold - A fold like the bellows of an accordion, forwards then backwards, in repeat.

B

Binding - The process of stitching or permanently adhering together a book.

C

Cartouche - An ornate or ornamental frame.

Chalking - A technique of coloring or aging paper by rubbing with chalk.

Chipboard - A thick cardboard available at art supply stores.

D

Decoupage - The art of decorating surfaces by applying paper cutouts and then coating with several layers of finish.

Dovetail - A flared end resembling a Dove's tail.

Die cut - To cut out around the edges of a print.

Debossing - The process of making designs or patterns in negative relief on paper. The opposite of *Embossing*.

Damask - Refers to a fabric of silk, wool, linen, or cotton, with a distinct pattern formed by the weaving.

E

Embossing - The process of making designs or patterns in relief on paper.

Engraving - A printing process in which fine lines are cut in wood or a metal plate to reproduce art.

G

Grommet - A small, metal eyelet used to fasten papers.

Glassine - A thin, dense, transparent or semitransparent paper highly resistant to air and grease. Glassine envelopes are typically used to protect photographs or slides.

M

Miter - The edge of a piece of paper that has been beveled to meet with a smooth miter joint.

Motif - A design or a thematic element.

Mat Board - A type of thick board, typically used for matting and framing photographs,

Monogram - A symbol of a name or names, consisting typically of a letter or several letters together.

P

Pleating - In paper crafting, to resemble a fold in cloth made by doubling material over on itself.

Pigment Ink - Refers to ink used in rubber stamping with a thick consistency and rich color. Pigment inks will not dry on glossy surfaces.

Papier Maché - A light, strong molding material of paper pulped with glue.

Paper Tole - A technique of layering paper to create depth and dimension.

Q

Quilt - In paper crafts this refers to attaching or covering with lines or patterns like those used in sewn quilts.

Quadrant Paper - Decorative paper divided into four distinct patterns or colors.

R

Rubber Stamp - A stamp made of rubber used for making imprints and reproducing artwork.

Reverse Decoupage - The art of decorating surfaces by applying paper cutouts to the back of a transparent surface.

S

Stylus - An instrument, usually with a pointed, or ball-point end, used for scoring or embossing paper.

Seam Binding Ribbon - A type of ribbon traditionally used in sewing.

Sleeve - Paper that has been folded and secured to hold a card or invitation.

T

Triangle - An instrument used to draw right angles.

Toile - Refers to a French pictorial textile pattern.

V

Vellum - Translucent or semi-translucent paper or card stock.

W

Watermark - A marking in paper usually produced by the pressure of projecting a design onto the paper processing roll and visible when the paper is held up to the light.

Weaving - The process of forming a texture, fabric, or design by interlacing or intertwining elements.

Index

About Anna Griffin

Having grown up in a family of artists, Anna Griffin's inclination toward graphic design is no surprise. Her talent, combined with her love of antiques, textiles, and prints, inspired her company's success and remarkable growth.

As a graduate in Environmental Design from North Carolina State University's School of Design, Griffin launched her business in 1994, creating one-of-a-kind handmade wedding and event invitations. Her custom invitation designs filled a void in the wedding industry, offering a much-needed alternative to the traditional engraved invitation.

In 1996, the business expanded to include a wholesale division, and Griffin introduced her first "imprintable" invitation with a custom look. People could now buy a box of invitations at a stationery store, print them at home, and have a result as elegant as a custom-designed product. Her signature vellum, combined with her use of antique engravings, botanicals, and fabrics gave her products a unique look and began an industry trend. Though the line has expanded to include a variety of products, Griffin's design philosophy remains constant: "I want people to look at our products and experience beauty. I want people to open my invitations and feel they've received a gift."

In 1998, the Griffin product line expanded to include a collection of elegant note cards, note pads, and greeting cards. *The Writing Papers Collection* quickly became a favorite with upscale gift stores, antiques stores, and garden shops, and the products have been featured in *Victoria* and *Martha Stewart Living* magazines.

In 2001, the line grew to include *Anna Griffin Home Office*, which includes beautiful file folders, mailing labels, guest books, and address books. "With the growing trend in the workforce to work at home," explains Griffin, "I saw the need for beautiful desk accessories to enhance one's personal workspace."

Also in 2001, the company launched *Anna Griffin Decorative Papers*, a line of beautiful papers, frames, and albums for the scrapbook market that offers consumers beautiful, high quality, unique papers in colorful botanicals, solids, stripes, and tone-on-tone patterns for making beautiful pages. There are also die cut frames, Victorian image die cuts, journaling pages, and albums.

Currently, Griffin appears on *DIY scrapbooking*, demonstrating her techniques for creating extraordinary scrapbook pages and has her own show, *Elegant Paper Crafting*, on QVC.